LEARN
TOUCH TYPING

In 12 Simple Lessons

Save ① Hour Per Day
[40 Hours per Month]

Muhammad Umar

Third Edition, 2021

ISBN: 9781729483046

Phone: +92(0)3149090001

Email: info@typing12.com

Website: Typing12.com

SOCIAL MEDIA

Facebook.com/TouchTyping12Lessons

Twitter.com/Typing12Lessons

Instagram.com/TouchTyping12Lessons

Pinterest.com/TouchTyping12Lessons

+92(0)3149090001

TouchTyping.tumblr.com

DEDICATION

I dedicate this book to my father and brother.

CONTENTS

CHAPTER 1

INTRODUCTION TO TOUCH TYPING

TOUCH TYPING

The process of *typing* without looking at the keyboard is known as *Touch Typing*. It involves typing with eight fingers and a thumb. In order to touch type properly, the fingers are required to be placed on the keys assigned to them.

Do not panic about fingers' location. Regular practice will *help* your fingers *learn* their *location* on the keyboard through muscle memory.

This *book* will *provide* you with more *tips and tricks* to learn or improve the touch-typing skill without using typing software.

ADVANTAGES OF TOUCH TYPING

There are a number of advantages of touch typing for anyone who aims to learn. The list below describes a few basic benefits.

1. Speed

Speed is considered the most essential and big advantage of learning to touch type. The normal speed of a touch typist is above 75-80 words per minute, while a hunt and peck typist would hardly reach 25 or 30 words per minute. Finding the next key for each stroke will definitely decrease your typing speed.

2. Accuracy

Accuracy is an equally important aspect and benefit of touch typing. If a typist can type more than 100 words per minute but there is no accuracy in his typing then such kind of typing skill is useless. No one will bother to try such typing services.

3. Fatigue

It is a matter of fact that typing is an exhausting activity for a long period of time. It makes a typist feel tired both mentally and physically. Touch typing reduces fatigue and makes you free to focus on two things at the same time. Another advantage in this regard is that touch typing relieves you from bending your head over the keyboard in order to find your next keystrokes.

4. Saving Time

Touch typing helps save time, it improves your typing speed e.g. from 30 to 60 words per minute. Essentially, it will take half time to do the same amount of work.

The following table describes how a touch typist performs better than a two-finger typist.

TYPIST	WORDS	MINUTES
Two fingers Typist	15	1
Average Typist	38	1
Touch Typist	75	1

5. Health

People who work on the keyboard or computer full day are likely to be a victim of various health issues such as repetitive stress injuries, or RSI. But do not worry, touch typing is here to help you. With touch typing you are not bent at keyboard and utilizing all fingers truly reduces risks RSI and other health issues.

6. Job Prospects

Typing is no more an optional skill. Many employers require computer skills and a certain typing speed to even consider someone for a position. Remember, hunt and peck typists are not preferred even if they can type 20-35 words in a minute. Learning touch typing can be one of the most valuable skills of career. It can help you in getting an entry job and then excel on it to the next level.

7. Attention

When typing with two fingers, the attention is divided between two things; finding the keys on the keyboard and doing work on the computer. It is human nature that he/she can pay attention to only one thing at a time. That's why touch-typing lets you focus on one thing instead of two. This has a tendency to increase output and make it easier to focus on the details of the project rather than having to find your keystrokes.

8. Editing

When you are typing with two fingers, you will not notice any spelling or grammar mistakes till you have made them. Touch typing allows you to edit and fix any spelling or grammar mistakes as you go. During typing, you can easily use the backspace key to fix them.

9. Save 20-40 Hours/month

With the help of touch typing, you can type faster and can save between 15 and 30 hours per month. Of course, you will have more time for your family and working less.

10. Avoid RSI and inflammation

You should know that bad typing technique can cause painful RSI and inflammation. Touch typing will help you fix these problems and can save your fingers.

11. Effectiveness

Research shows that faster typists are more effective. They can perform 2-3 times better in communication and social media.

12. Computer Savvy

Your fast typing skills will definitely save a lot of work at the office. You will be known as computer savvy and people will be amazed at your typing speed and efficiency. It happened many times, when someone observes me typing so fast, they are impressed and then ask me how they can also learn touch typing skills.

TYPES OF TYPIST

Hmm... sounds funny "**types of typist**", but they do exist in today's computer age. The preceding section describes the different level of typist which will help you to determine what type of typist you are. You may fall under one or more categories under certain circumstances.

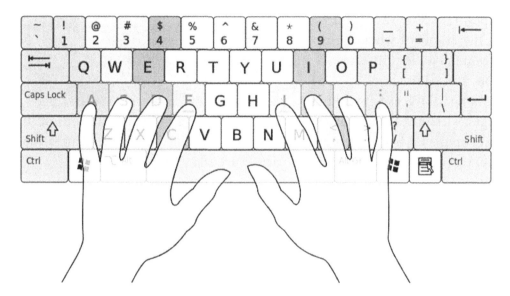

Beginner

A touch-typing beginner is not familiar with QWERTY keyboard layout. You have to first know the nuts and bolts of touch typing. Reading and following this book "Learn Touch Typing in 12 Simple Lessons" will help you familiarize yourself with touch typing quickly. Do regular practice of minimum one hour to achieve your goals. Focus on every key as you type and remember the position of the finger on the keyboard.

Hunt Peck Typist

A hunt peck typist is the one who is familiar with most keys and their location on the keyboard. He /she generally uses only one or two fingers to type. Besides, he/she also looks at the keyboard when typing. If you fall under this category, you can quit hunting and pecking habits easily by taking  regular lessons daily because you already know the different positions of the keys on the keyboard. Remember hunting and pecking not only reduces your typing speed but also has a bad impact on accuracy.

Touch Typist

In my opinion, most people fall into this category. Maybe are also in love with touch typing. In touch typing, the typist can type all the alphabetic and certain punctuation keys without looking at the keyboard. But at the same time when a touch typist types numbers and symbols (signs) he/she might look at the keyboard. The odd thing about a touch typist is that he uses all his fingers when typing. You can achieve the next level by concentrating and practicing only numbers and symbols key on the top row.

Full Keyboard Touch Typist

A full keyboard touch typist is one who uses all fingers to type all most keys including numbers and symbols without looking at the keyboard. This kind of typist can type very fast with great accuracy, typing fast and accurately can help achieve high performance and productivity.

TYPING SPEED AND ITS MEASUREMENT

Typing speed refers to how quickly a person can type alphabetical characters with the help of a keyboard.

Typing speed is measured in Words Per Minute (WPM) or roughly Characters Per Minute (CPM). In certain situations, words per hour (WPH) or key depression per minute (DHM) are some of the units used to track down the progress of typing.

The standard length of a word is five characters including space and punctuation signs. In simple words, WPM determines how many words can be typed in one minute. 38-40 words per minute is considered an average typing speed.

A fast typing speed is said to be 120 WPM with minimum errors. But there are still crazy typists who achieved a speed of 212 words. Barbara Blackburn is the name who earned the title of the fastest typist, typing 150 words in a minute and her top speed recorded was 212 words.

However, some people do not bother to know their typing speed. If you do not count yourself among them and are interested to know your typing speed, then follow this link.

Typing12.com/typing-speed-test

In mathematical language, typing speed is inversely proportional to accuracy which means as you gauge more speed you will lose accuracy. There are rare cases where high speed and great accuracy are reached at the same time. The basic reason behind this is that humans can concentrate on only one thing at a time.

CHARTS OF FINGERS

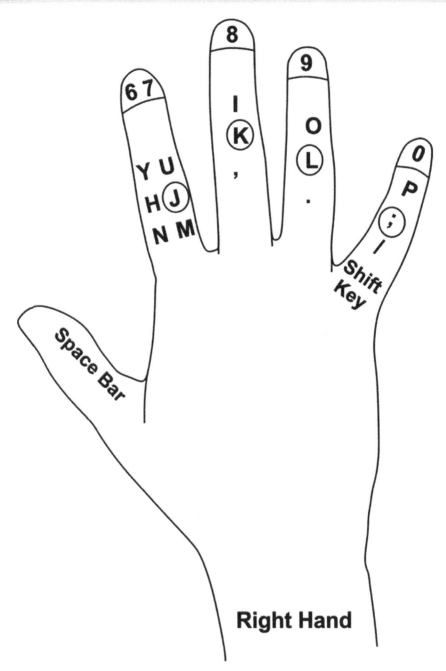

Figure 1: Right-hand chart

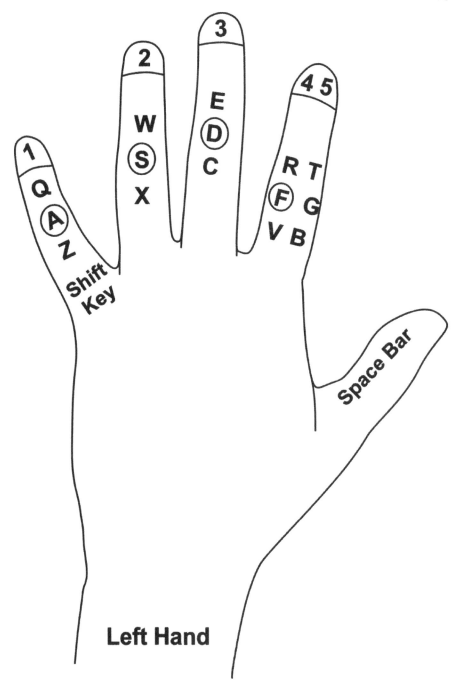

Figure 2: Left-hand chart

TYPING TUTOR SOFTWARE

Typing tutor is a type of software that helps you learn and improve typing skills by doing exercises, playing typing games, or taking typing tests. The typing exercises usually focus on alphabets, alphanumeric, punctuation, Shift keys, Enter, and Backspace keys.

Although there are some benefits of typing tutor software, you cannot trust it as the major player in attaining typing skills. Because in real life, you mostly type from a physical paper such as a book, magazine, or any other kind of printed document. The following are some supporting points to my claim:

❶ Using a typing tutor software, a user types by looking at the screen which makes the typist habitual of looking at the screen during typing. For such a typist, it is difficult to type from a real page. As a result, he or she cannot reach the desired typing speed and accuracy. Conversely, in practical life, one has to type from a page.

❷ In the case of typing tutor software, the possibility of errors is more than that of typing from a page. A typist makes more errors typing from the screen but feels comfortable with the page.

❸ By looking at the screen, if one makes an error, he tries to correct it immediately by pressing the "Backspace" or "Delete" key, which not only affects typing speed but also wastes time.

❹ Typing tutor software uses games for entertaining users. Although these games are designed to improve typing skills, they are actually a waste of time. In addition to this, before playing these games it is required to learn how to play them, which diverges the user's attention to something else. In the worst case, typing tutor software is only used for playing games.

5 The User Interface of typing tutor software is often very complicated. A user may face problems by using such typing tutor software. Once, I was teaching a lesson on typing tutor software to one of my classes and the topic was "How to use a certain Typing Tutor Software". Believe me, I tried a few times, but I failed to start the typing lesson. Then I guided my students to another typing tutor software which comparatively had an easy interface.

6 If a typing tutor software corrupts or crashes, the user's data i.e., progress reports, practiced exercises, and the account will be lost. The user will not have any idea about the exercises he has practiced so far. He might not really remember from which exercise he has to start.

7 Obviously, a good typing tutor software carries a cost. An ordinary user may not be able to purchase a license for such expensive software. Although there are some freeware and open-source typing tutor software available in the market, they do not provide all the features.

You must be thinking that I have listed only disadvantages of typing tutor software and skipped its advantages. I got you. There are some advantages of typing tutor software as well for instance, Typing lessons & Exercises, Progress Tracking & Report, Accuracy and speed analysis, Games, Typing Tests, Multiple Users Accounts, Virtual Keyboard, Custom lessons etc. Remember, other than a few core features, the rest are optional and not required to learn typing skills.

NEVER RUSH FOR TYPING

Take it as a piece of advice, do not rush for touch typing skill. Typing is a skill that is learned by doing practice, by sitting at your computer and making friendship with the keyboard. By hurrying up, you cannot learn typing skill because it is not a concept or law to learn by heart quickly.

To put it simply, you can learn typing skill by doing hard work, investing time and making your hand dirty with the keyboard. Making your hand dirty with the keyboard means typing with the keyboard yourself.

Please note that it may take a little more time than you would expect, particularly if you have a bad experience to rework, but at end of the day, a small investment in terms of time will pay off in more benefits than you can imagine.

▸▸ **KEY POINTS**

- ✔ Do not worry about speed, it will increase as you do more practice.

- ✔ Take time to avoid typing errors. At an early stage, it is not bad if you take more time than expected.

- ✔ Read one or two words in advance.

- ✔ I am going to emphasize this point again that successful touch typing takes time and effort. There is nothing ingenious about it – strong determination and hard work will help to eliminate any distractions.

- ✔ If you feel tired or something starts to ache, it is the best idea to leave it for another time.

- ✔ Do your part honestly, you will be amazed at just how quickly your speed and accuracy will build up.

CHAPTER 2

GETTING STARTED

TOOLS REQUIRED FOR TOUCH TYPING

Before you start touch typing, you will need some basic tools.

- Desktop PC or Laptop
- Plain text editor (Notepad) or maybe Word Processing package (Microsoft Word, Libre office etc.)
- A good-sized desk
- An adjustable chair with a supporting backrest as shown in the *Figure 3*.
- Hand charts (Given page 12 and 13 of this book)

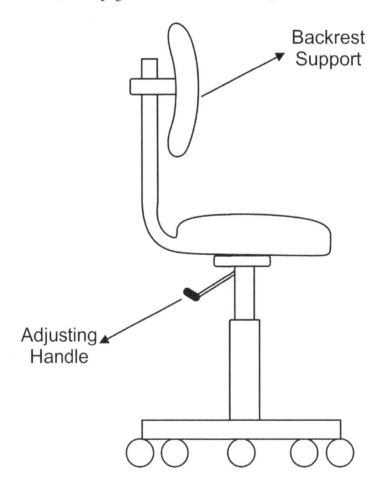

Figure 3: Chair with a backrest support

POSITIONING YOURSELF

Positioning yourself at your desk is an important task. How you position yourself at your desk will determine your comfort while typing. The correct position is shown in the Figure 4.

Make sure to position the following properly.

Sitting	1. Sit on the chair exactly in front of the monitor or LCD screen.
	2. When typing, do not move to the right or left.
	3. A correct position on the chair will not make you tired.
Head	1. Erect your head and look straight to the screen.
	2. Tilting your head forwards will put a stress on your neck.
	3. Remember, a poor head position can result in headaches.
Shoulders	1. Make sure that shoulders are at rest.
	2. Raising them up will make you tired very quickly and can cause serious shoulder problems.
Elbows	1. Keep elbows close to your body.
	2. When touch typing, do NOT rest elbows on armrests.
	3. Let your shoulders support elbows and arms.
Fingers	1. Curve your fingers but not too much. You will need to raise your fingers to type from top rows and bring down to type from bottom row.
	2. In the case of a laptop computer, you may need to raise more because the keys on a laptop are closer together and the keyboard itself is flatter.
Wrists	1. The wrists should be flat.
	2. Do not bend them and make sure there is a straight line from the knuckles of your middle fingers to your elbows.
Feet	1. The feet should be flat on the floor.
	2. Do not cross your legs.
	3. Erecting forward or keeping them under the chair will result in pain.

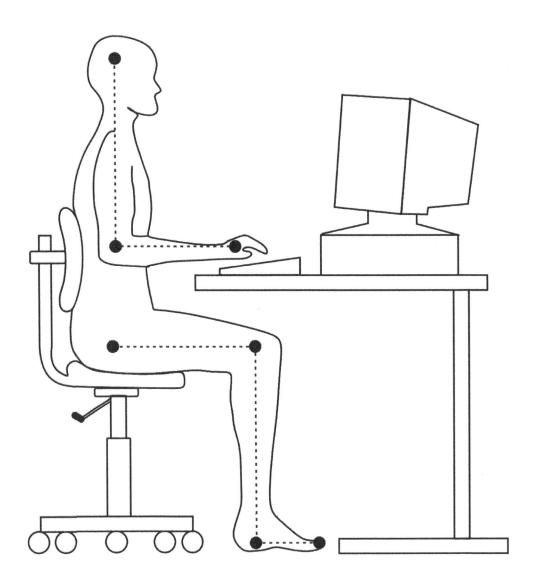

Figure 4: Positioning Yourself (Correct Position)

SUPPORTING STUFF

The following points can be very helpful for beginners.

Copyholder	If possible, use a copy holder. It holds paper for you and can stand on the desk or attached to the monitor. At first, placing the hand chart on the holder is a good idea but eventually, as you work you will not need a hand chart. Once you have memorized all the keys, use a copy holder to hold paper.
Lighting	Make sure the room lighting is proper. In case you are working in an office, there may be certain rules and regulations where you can position your equipment. At home, you may place your LCD (monitor) such that the window is behind it. Glare from either lighting or sunshine should be avoided. For safety, you can buy a filter to place on the monitor's screen. The filter may degrade the image quality a bit but can help in reducing strain on eyes.
Take Regular Breaks	Health is the most precious thing in the world. To have good health, take regular breaks about 10 minutes after every hour. If possible, you should walk around for a minute and come back.
Close your eyes for a while	As eyes are getting dried by continuous exposure to the monitor. Close your eyes for a few seconds which will help to clean and comfort your eyes. At least, slowly blink your eyes a few times. After every two years, visit an ophthalmologist or vision care for an eye checkup.
Arial font	Use the Arial font and 12-point size for all the practice lessons. It is a fixed font and each letter takes up the same amount of space, and your lines will all finish at the same point. For a clearer view of your work use double line spacing.

FINGERS ON KEYS

Home Row

The middle row of keys on the keyboard is referred to as "**Home**" row. The eight keys which start from left to right i.e. A, S, D, F, J, K, L, are known as "Home" keys. They are situated in the middle of the keyboard. The four fingers of the left hand are placed on A, S, D, and F (with the little finger on A) while the four fingers of the right hand are placed on J, K, L, and ; (with the little finger on ;)

Always hover your fingers over these eight keys and from this position you should type every other letter from the top or bottom row. You can also type numbers and symbols using the same method.

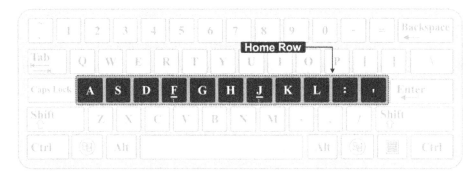

Bumps on F and J

Most keyboards have special bumps or nipples on F and J keys to help you position your left and right hand on the keyboard without looking at the keyboard.

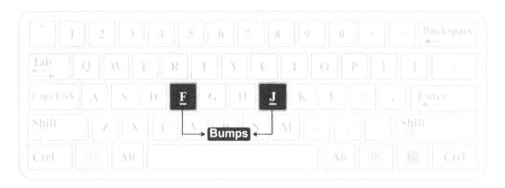

Top Row

The row just above the home row is called the "**Top**" row. It includes the keys Q, W, E, R, T, Y, U, I, O, P, P, [,], \. You have to raise your fingers to type letters from the top row.

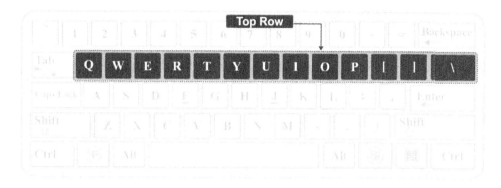

Bottom Row

The row just below the home row is called the "**Bottom**" row. It includes the keys Z, X, C, V, B, N, M, , . . You have to bring down fingers to type letters from the bottom row.

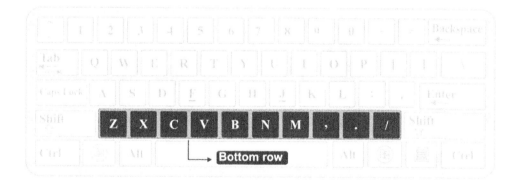

Home Column

Each finger is used for a vertical column of keys, which you may call as a "**Home column**". Keep in mind that a column is not straight up or down, but rather slopes up to the left or right.

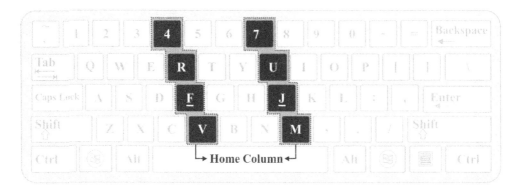

Index Fingers

Both index fingers are required to take care of an additional column, the one next to their home columns towards the middle of the keyboard. The **F** finger is responsible for additional keys i.e. **B, G, T,5** and in similar way **J** finger is responsible for **N, H, Y,6**

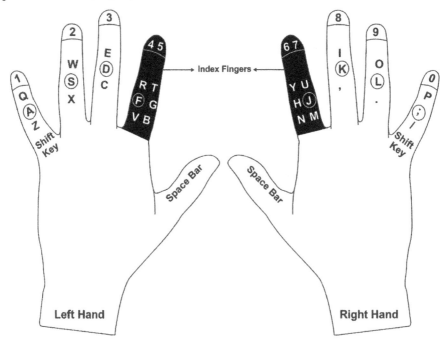

24

Thumbs

To press Spacebar, use the right or left thumb if you are right-handed or left-handed respectively. Some people use the thumb of whatever hand is more convenient for them. The thumbs can also be used for the "Windows" key on PC and "Command" key on Apple computer.

Pinkies (little fingers)

Although, pinkies are small but are required to perform more in touch typing. The left-hand pinky has to type all keys on the left side of its home column i.e. Escape, Tilde, Tab, Caps Lock, Shift, Ctrl, and other keys. In similar fashion, the right-hand pinky is responsible for all the keys on the left side of its home column.

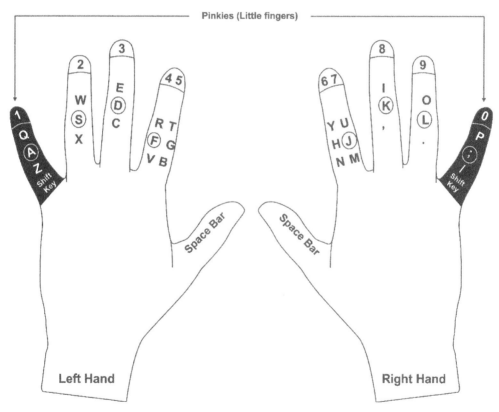

KEYS ASSOCIATION WITH FINGERS IN A CONCISE WAY

There are about 101 keys on a standard keyboard. Each finger from both hands is responsible for typing one or more letters or symbol. In addition to this, number from 0 to 9 are also assigned to different fingers.

The following tables solve the mystery of fingers and keys association in a concise way.

Finger	Alphabet	Alpha numeric / symbol	Control keys
Lady	Y, U, H, Ⓙ, N, M	6,7, ^, &	-
Middle	I, Ⓚ , ,	8, *	-
Ring	O, Ⓛ, .	9, (	-
Little	P, (;),/	0, -, =,), _, +, [, ',], \, {, }, |, :, ", ?	Shift, Ctrl, Enter, Backspace, Delete
Thumb			Space bar, Alt, Windows, Fn key

Table for Right Hand

Finger	Alphabet	Alpha numeric / symbol	Control keys
Lady	R, T, Ⓕ, G,V,B	4,5,$,%	-
Middle	E, Ⓓ,C	3,#	-
Ring	W,Ⓢ, X	2,@	-
Little	Q,Ⓐ ,Z	1,`,!,~	Shift, Ctrl, Tab, Caps lock
Thumb	-	-	Space bar, Alt, Windows, Fn key

Table for left hand

The circle *enclosed letter* indicates the '*Home*' key. Sit your fingers smoothly on these fingers and take up or down to type any letter from the top or bottom row, respectively.

To type a capital letter, hold down the shift key with the pinky of the alternate hand. For instance, hold down the right shift key with right hand pinky to type capital "S" letter. Most of the controls keys such as control (Ctrl), Shift, Backspace, Enter, Delete and shift keys are assigned to little finger (pinky).

 ▶▶ KEY POINTS

- It is important that the fingers are always kept on the "Home" keys.

- As you type, say the letters to yourself.

- Avoid getting into bad habits by pressing the wrong key for the letter you are typing.

- Look at the hand chart whenever you get lost but do not look at the keys or your fingers.

- Observe your posture and make an adjustment if you are in the wrong position in terms of feet, elbow, or wrists etc.

- Press keys only with the fingers for which they have been reserved.

- After typing another letter or number, reposition your fingers on home keys i.e. ASDF – JKL;

- When typing, think of the location of the symbol on the keyboard.

- During typing, your keystrokes should come at equal intervals by maintaining a rhythm.

- The SHIFT key is always pressed by the pinky (little) finger opposite to the one hitting the other key. For example, if you want to type capital A, first hold down shift with right pinky and then press A key.

- Focus on ring fingers and pinky fingers because they are greatly underdeveloped.

- As a rule of touch typing, type each line until it is finished and most importantly type it without looking at the keyboard or fingers. As discussed earlier, at first each line may take many tries, but keep reminding yourself that patience is the key.

CHAPTER 3

PRACTICE LESSONS 1 TO 4

IN THIS CHAPTER

▶▶ Lesson 1

- KEYS ➤ A , S , D , F , J , K , L

▶▶ Lesson 2

- KEYS ➤ E , I , G , H

▶▶ Lesson 3

- KEYS ➤ O , N , Shift , T

▶▶ Lesson 4

- KEYS ➤ Y , .

LESSON 1

KEYS ➤ A , S , D , F , J , K , L

Note:

- Type only the text, do not type the line number shown in the gray color.
- **Do not** use Backspace or Delete key.
- When a line ends, **press** Enter key using the right little finger.

1. aaa aas aad aaf asa ass asd asf ada ads add adf afa afs afd aff

2. saa sas sad saf ssa sss ssd ssf sda sds sdd sdf sfa sfs sfd sff

3. daa das dad daf dsa dss dsd dsf dda dds ddd ddf dfa dfs dfd dff

4. faa fas fad faf fsa fss fsd fsf fda fds fdd fdf ffa ffs ffd fff fdsa asdf

5. fdsa asdf fdsa asdf fdsa asdf fdsa asdf fdsa asdf dfsa asdf dfas

6. jjj jjk jjl jj; jkj jkk jkl jk; jlj jlk jll jl; j;j j;k j;l j;; kjj kjk kjl kj; kkj kkk kkl a

7. kk; klj klk kll kl; k;j k;k k;l k;; ljj ljk ljl lj; lkj lkk lkl lk; llj llk lll ll; l;j l;k l;l

8. l;; ;jj ;jk ;jl ;j; ;kj ;kk ;kl ;k; ;lj ;lk ;ll ;l; ;;j ;;k ;;l ;;; jjj jj; jkj lkk ;;j ;;k ;;l l;l

9. jkl; ;lkj jkl; ;lkj jkl; ;lkj jkl; ;lkj jkl; ;lkj l k;; ljj ljk ljl ;;j ;;k ;;l ;;j ;;k

10. aaj aak aal aa; asa ass asd asf asj ask asl as; ada ads add adf

11. adj adk adl ad; afa afs afd aff afj afk afl af; aja ajs ajd ajf ajj ajk

12. ajl aj; aka aks akd akf akj akk akl ak; ala als ald alf alj alk all al;

13. a;a a;s a;d a;f a;j a;k a;l a;; saa sas sad saf saj sak sal sa; ssa

29

14.   sss ssd ssf ssj ssk ssl ss; sda sds sdd sdf sdj sdk sdl sd; sfa sfs

15.   sfd sff sfj sfk sfl sf; sja sjs sjd sjf sjj sjk sjl sj; ska sks skd skf skj

16.   skk skl sk; sla sls sld slf slj slk sll sl; s;a s;s s;d s;f s;j s;k s;l s;;

17.   daa das dad daf daj dak dal da; dsa dss dsd dsf dsj dsk dsl ds;

18.   dda dds ddd ddf ddj ddk ddl dd; dfa dfs dfd dff dfj dfk dfl df; dja

19.   djs djd djf djj djk djl dj; dka dks dkd dkf dkj dkk dkl dk; dla dls dld

20.   dlf dlj dlk dll dl; d;a d;s d;d d;f d;j d;k d;l d;; faa fas fad faf faj fak

21.   fal fa; fsa fss fsd fsf fsj fsk fsl fs; fda fds fdd fdf fdj fdk fdl fd; ffa ffs

22.   ffd fff ffj ffk ffl ff; fja fjs fjd fjf fjj fjk fjl fj; fka fks fkd fkf fkj fkk fkl fk;

23.   fla fls fld flf flj flk fll fl; f;a f;s f;d f;f f;j f;k f;l f;; jaa jas jad jaf jaj jak

24.   jal ja; jsa jss jsd jsf jsj jsk jsl js; jda jds jdd jdf jdj jdk jdl jd; jfa jfs

25.   jfd jff jfj jfk jfl jf; jja jjs jjd jjf jjj jjk jjl jj; jka jks jkd jkf jkj jkk jkl jk; jla

26.   jls jld jlf jlj jlk jll jl; j;a j;s j;d j;f j;j j;k j;l j;; kaa kas kad kaf kaj kak

27.   kal ka; ksa kss ksd ksf ksj ksk ksl ks; kda kds kdd kdf kdj kdk kdl

28.   kd; kfa kfs kfd kff kfj kfk kfl kf; kja kjs kjd kjf kjj kjk kjl kj; kka kks

29.   kkd kkf kkj kkk kkl kk; kla kls kld klf klj klk kll kl; k;a k;s k;d k;f k;j

30.   k;k k;l k;; laa las lad laf laj lak lal la; lsa lss lsd lsf lsj lsk lsl ls; lda

31.   lds ldd ldf ldj ldk ldl ld; lfa lfs lfd lff lfj lfk lfl lf; lja ljs ljd ljf ljj ljk ljl lj;

32.   lka lks lkd lkf lkj lkk lkl lk; lla lls lld llf llj llk lll ll; l;a l;s l;d l;f l;j l;k l;l

33.   l;; ;aa ;as ;ad ;af ;aj ;ak ;al ;a; ;sa ;ss ;sd ;sf ;sj ;sk ;sl ;s; ;da ;ds

34.   ;dd ;df ;dj ;dk ;dl ;d; ;fa ;fs ;fd ;ff ;fj ;fk ;fl ;f; ;ja ;js ;jd ;jf ;jj ;jk ;jl ;j;

35.   ;ka ;ks ;kd ;kf ;kj ;kk ;kl ;k; ;la ;ls ;ld ;lf ;lj ;lk ;ll ;l; ;;a ;;s ;;d ;;f ;;j ;;k

36.   skald flask lads flak fads dals dal ads kas las sad ask fad ska

LESSON 2

KEYS ➤ E , I , G , H

Note:

- To type the letter "**e**", raise the **D** finger to the top row and type it.
- To type the letter "**i**", raise the **K** finger to the top row and type it.
- To type the letter "**g**", move the **F** finger to the adjacent key and type it.
- To type the letter "**h**", move the **J** finger to the adjacent key and type it.

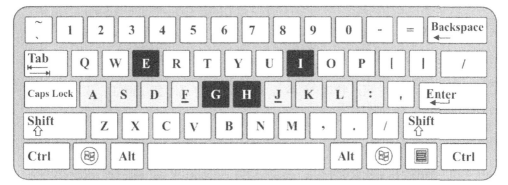

1. eee eei eeg eeh eie eii eig eih ege egi egg egh ehe ehi ehg ehh

2. iee iei ieg ieh iie iii iig iih ige igi igg igh ihe ihi ihg ihh gee gei geg

3. geh gie gii gig gih gge ggi ggg ggh ghe ghi ghg ghh hee hei heg

4. heh hie hii hig hih hge hgi hgg hgh hhe hhi hhg hhh eeg egh ihg

5. adf adj adk adl ad; ade adi adg adh afa afs afd aff afj afk afl af;

6. a;i a;g a;h aea aes aed aef aej aek ael ae; aee aei aeg aeh aia

7. sai sag sah ssa sss ssd ssf ssj ssk ssl ss; sse ssi ssg ssh sda

8. sld slf slj slk sll sl; sle sli slg slh s;a s;s s;d s;f s;j s;k s;l s;; s;e s;i

9. s;g s;h sea ses sed sef sej sek sel se; see sei seg seh sia sis sid

10. dss dsd dsf dsj dsk dsl ds; dse dsi dsg dsh dda dds ddd ddf ddj

11. dfg dfh dja djs djd djf djj djk djl dj; dje dji djg djh dka d;l d;; d;e d;i

12. d;g d;h dea des ded def dej dek del de; dee dei deg deh dia dis

13. did dif dij dik dil di; die dii faa fas fad faf faj fak fal fa; fae fai fag

31

14. fsa fss fsd fsf fsj fsk fsl fs; fse fsi fsg fsh fda fds fdd fdf fdj fdk fdl

15. f;j f;k f;l f;; f;e f;i f;g f;h fea fes fed fgh fha fhs fhd fhf fhj fhk fhl fh;

16. fhe fhi fhg fhh jaa jas jad jaf jaj jak jal ja; jae jai jag jah jsa jss jsd

17. jgg jgh jha jhs jhd jhf jhj jhk jhl jh; jhe jhi jhg jhh kaa kas kad kaf

18. kaj kak kal ka; kae kai kfd kff kfj kfk kfl kf; kfe kfi kfg kfh kja kjs

19. kig kih kga kgs kgd kgf kgj kgk kgl kg; lss lsd lsf lsj lsk lsl ls; lse

20. lsi lsg lsh lda lds ldd ldf ldj ldk ldl ld; lde ldi ldg ldh lfa lfs lfd lff lfj

21. lfk lfl lf; lfe lfi lfg l;a l;s l;d l;f l;j l;k l;l l;; l;e l;i l;g l;h lea les led lef lej

22. lek lel le; lee lei leg leh lia lis lid lif lij lik lil li; lie lii lig lih ;is ;id ;if ;ij

23. ;ik ;il ;i; ;ie ;ii ;ig ;ih ;ga ;gs ;gd ;gf ;gj ;gk ;gl ;g; ;ge ;gi ;gg ;gh ;ha

24. ;hs ;hd ;hf ;hj ;hk ;hl ;h; ;he ;hi ;hg ;hh eaa eas ead eaf eaj eak

25. eal ea; eae eai eag eah esa ess esd esf esj esk esl es; ese esi

26. ek; eke eki ekg ekh ela els eld elf elj elk ell el; ele eli elg elh e;a

27. eel ee; eee eei eeg eeh eia eis eid eif ehe ehi ehg ehh iaa ias

28. isg ish ida ids idd ikd ikf ikj ikk ikl ik; ike iki ikg ikh ila ils ild ilf ilj ilk

29. iek iel ie; iee iei ieg ieh iia iis iid iif iij iik iil ii; iie iii iig iih iga igs igd

30. igf igj igk igl ig; ige igi igg igh iha ihs ihd ihf ihj ihk ihl ih; ihe ihi ihg

31. ihh gaa gas gad gaf gaj gak gal ga; gae gai gag gah gsa gss gsd

32. gd; gde gdi gdg gdh gfa gfs gfd gff gfj gfk gfl gf; gfe gfi gfg gfh

33. gkl gk; gke gki gkg gkh gla gls gld glf glj glk gll gl; gle gli glg glh

34. g;a g;s g;d g;f g;j g;k g;l g;; g;e g;i g;g g;h gea ges ged gef gej

35. gek gel ge; gee gei geg geh gia gis gid gif gij gik gil gi; gie gii gig

36. hsg hsh hda hds hdd hdf hdj hdk hdl hd; hde hdi hdg hdh hfa hfs

37. hfd hff hfj hfk hfl hf; hfe hfi hfg hfh hja hjs hjd hjf hjj hjk hjl hj; hje

38. hld hlf hlj hlk hll hl; hle hli hlg hlh h;a h;s h;d h;f h;j h;k h;l h;; h;e

39. his hid hif hij hik hil hi; hie hii hig hih hga hgs hgd hgf hgj hgk hgl

40.   hg; hge hgi hgg hgh hha hhs hhd hhf hhj hhk hhl hh; hhe hhi hhg

41.   gadflies dealfish flashed deafish halides khalifs flaked dad feed

42.   glades shield fields glides jadish jailed gashed geisha ligase has

43.   fished failed jihads khalif jehads alsike deasil dad falsie elfish did

44.   halide slaked afield silage hailed ideals said lashed sighed felids

45.   ladies aisled alkies flags fails flags flags fails flash flake flask sad

46.   khadi hikes felid false filed files field fakes lades faked fleas hails

47.   ideas idles dad hades jades glide hajes ideal hajis hides heals

48.   heads hiked hales haled hakes gales kales isled flies flied glade

49.   gilds jails jakes jehad jihad gelid flesh shake had slide alike likes

50.   liked algid sidle aside degas dales has shade sheaf dashi deals

51.   deash sheik shelf asked have shied shale dikes aegis leaks said

52.   lakes slake lased agile leads skied lakhs ailed aisle skald fades

53.   delis jade dad sled shed shea jags jail slid side idea hila ides idle

54.   sild silk ilka hide skeg isle skid sigh lake kids legs lies life lakh

55.   laid lase lags lads lash lade lead leaf like leis seal sail self jigs

56.   shad sale kale safe kegs sage said keas sake flak flag fish file

57.   fila figs deal fids flea fled gash gals gale dale dals gads dash

58.   dad feds elhi diel dies egis digs egad dish disk dial elks dhal deli

59.   fake fail fads desk edhs dais held hags seed aids ails ales hail

60.   haji hake heil fade aged heal head ages half hale aide hade geld

61.   dahl gels deaf glad did dahs gild glia ski sad dal die dig she dis

62.   age ads sei seg sea ale del ail ask ska ash sag dah ids fed gas

63.   gadflies dealfish flashed deafish halides khalifs flaked dad feed

64.   fished failed jihads khalif jehads alsike deasil dad falsie elfish did

65.   ladies aisled alkies flags fails flags flags fails flash flake flask sad

LESSON 3

KEYS ➤ O , N , Shift , T

Note:

- To type the letter "**o**", raise the **L** finger to the top row and type it.
- To type the letter "**n**", bring down the **J** finger to the bottom row and type it.

- To type a letter in capital, you can use **Shift** keys. There are two shift keys; one for the right hand and the other for the left hand. The rule is to use the right-hand **Shift** key when typing a letter with the left hand and vice versa.

- To type the letter "**t**", raise the **F** finger to the top row and type it.

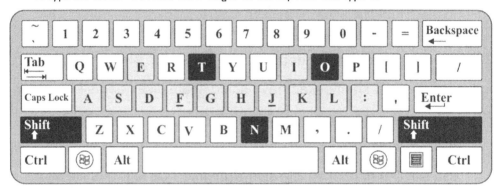

1. ooo oon oot ono onn ont oto otn ott noo non not nno nnn nnt
2. OOO OON OOT ONO ONN ONT OTO OTN OTT NOO NON
3. nto ntn ntt too ton tot tno tnn tnt tto ttn ttt nto ntn ntt nnn nnt
4. NOT NNO NNN NNT NTO NTN NTT TOO TON TOT TNO NO
5. ooo ooN oot ooA oos ooD ooF ooj ook ooL oo oo oNo oNN
6. oNt oNA oNs oND oNF oNj oNk oNL oN oN oto otN ott otA ots
7. otD otF otj otk otL ot ot oAo oAN oAt oAA oAs oAD oAF oAj
8. oAk oAL oj oj oko okN okt okA oks okD okF okj okk okL ok ok
9. oLo oLN oLt oLA oLs oLD oLF oLj oLk oLL oL oL o o o N o t o
10. A o s o D o F o j o k o L o   o oo oN ot oA os oD oF oj ok oL o
11. o Noo NoN Not NoA Nos NoD NoF Noj Nok NoL No No NNo

12. NNN NNt NNA NNs NND NNF NNj NNk NNL NN NN Nto NA

13. Nso NsN Nst NsA Nss NsD NsF Nsj Nsk NsL Ns Ns NDo NDN

14. NDt NDA NDs NDD NDF NDj NDk N N too toN tot toA tos toD

15. toF toj tok toL to to tNo tNN tNt tNA tNs tND tNF tNj tNk tNL tN

16. tN tFD tFF tFj tFk tFL tF tF tjo tjN tjt tjA tjs tjD tjF tjj tjk tjL tj tj

17. tko tkN tkt tkA tks tkD tkF tkj tkk tkL tk tk tLo tLN tLt tLA tLs tLD

18. tA ts tD tF tj tk tL t t Aoo AoN Aot AoA Aos AoD AoF Aoj Aok

19. AoL Ao Ao ANo ANN ANt ANA ANs AND ANF ANj ANk ANL

20. AN AN Ato AtN Att AtA Ats AtD AtF Atj Atk AtL At At AAo AAN

21. AAt AAA AAs AAD AAF AAj AAk AAL AA AA Aso AsN Ast

22. AsA Ass AsD AsF Asj Ask AsL As As ADo ADN ADt ADA ADs

23. ADD ADF ADj ADk ADL AD AD AFo AFN AFt AFA AFs AFD

24. AFF AFj AFk AFL AF AF Ajo AjN Ajt AjA Ajs AjD AjF Ajj Ajk

25. AjL Aj Aj Ako AkN Akt AkA Aks AkD AkF Akj Akk AkL Ak Ak

26. ALo ALN ALt ALA ALs ALD ALF ALj ALk ALL AL AL A o A N A

27. t A A A s A D A F A j A k A L A A Ao AN At AA As AD AF Aj

28. Ak AL A A soo soN sot soA sos soD soF soj sok soL so so

29. sNo sNN sNt sNA sNs sND sNF DFD DFF DFj DFk DFL DF

30. DF Djo DjN Djt DjA Djs DjD DjF Djj Djk DjL Dj Dj Dko DkN Dkt

31. DkA Dks DkD DkF Dkj Dkk DkL Dk Dk DLo DLN DLt DLA DLs

32. DLD DLF DLj DLk DLL DL DL D o D N D t D A D s D D D F D j

33. Fot FoA Fos FoD FoF Foj Ftk FtL Ft Ft FAo FAN FAt FAA FAs

34. FAD FAF FAj FAk FAL FA FA Fso FsN Fst FsA Fss FsD FsF

35. Fsj Fsk FsL Fs Fs FDo FDN FDt FDA FDs FDD FDF FDj FDk

36. FDL FD FD FFo FFN FFt FFA FFs FFD FFF FFj FFk FFL FF

37. FF Fjo FjN Fjt FjA Fjs FjD FjF Fjj Fjk FjL Fj Fj Fko FkN Fkt FkA

38. Fks FkD FkF Fkj Fkk FkL Fk Fk FLo FLN FLt FLA FLs FLD

39. FLF FLj FLk FLL FL FL F o F N F t F A F s F D F F F j F k F L

40. joD joF joj jok joL jo jo jNo jNN jNt jNA jNs jND jNF jNj jNk jNL

41. jN jN jto jtN jtt jtA jts jtD jtF jtj jtk jtL jt jt jAo jAN jAt jAA jAs jAD

42. jAF jAj jAk jAL jA jA jso jsN Ask; See; Don; Fog; Gas; Had;

43. Defoliant Athelings Fashioned Deflation Fanlights Desalting

44. Deflating Eightfold Alongside Angelfish Giltheads Gatefolds

45. Flagstone Hosteling Hailstone Ghostlike Halftones Safelight

46. Insolated Longheads Legations Longhead Insolate Kinglets

47. Inflated Leadings Lightens Loadings Leashing Legation

48. Loathing Latigoes Knighted Hotlines Jostling Linkages Inflates

49. Lankiest Isolated Flakiest Goatfish Goatskin Good Goldfish

50. Halftone Halogens Flashing Gilthead Foliaged Flokatis Foliated

51. Floating Gadflies Gasoline Gatefold Flighted Gelatins Gelation

52. Fleshing Genitals Handiest Headlong Finagled Finagles

53. Holdings Headings Holdfast Hedonist Handlist Hidalgos

54. Foliates Delights Diastole Diagnose Fanglike Atheling Fanlight

55. Delating Feltings Alighted Adjoints Feasting Deashing Dealings

56. Dealfish Adhesion Elations Astonied Fatlings Toadfish Toenails

57. Stalking Signaled Softhead Shafting Sodalite Shingled

58. Shoaling Stealing Shinleaf Slighted Talkings Neoliths Songlike

59. Sinkhole Tangelos Steading Sedating Sedation Skinhead

60. Sidelong Olefins Thanked Teasing Skating Stoking Tenfold

61. Singled Shitake Shoaled Sighted Singlet Shoeing Tangles

62. Shingle Tangoed Salient Tangled Talkies Sandhog Seating

63. Tangelo Talking Sainted Takings Onstage Shifted Sandlot

64. Tasking Shanked Shaking Shafted Shading Sealing Staking

65. Slinked Sleight Slating Staling Slaking Stalked Soaking Slanted

66. Soilage Skatole Salting Neolith Stained Stifled Slanged Elastin

67. Doeskin Doglike Dogfish Doltish Anisole Enfolds Donates

68. Anethol Dotages Eloigns Elation Easting Elating Dingoes

69. Dingles Dilates Delight Dankest Defiant Defangs Dangles

70. Dealing Denials Anklets Diglots Dialogs Antilog Antlike Detains

71. Details Dentils Dentals Deafish Fashion Eoliths Fanlike

72. Fantods Felting Fasting Dashing Fatlike Ethanol Fatling

73. Etalons Aiglets Fainted Fanjets Agonist Alights Fidgets English

74. Aligned Adjoins Adjoint Entails Agonies Jangles Leaking

75. Jangled Keloids Loathes Latigos Loathed Isolate Loafing

76. Leading Loading Leafing Leasing Lengths Lentigo Lighten

77. Lighted Ligates Lentoid Ligated Jointed Ligands Jostled

78. Joshing Legions Kalends Jingoes Leftish Jesting Linkage

79. Joisted Lingoes Kalongs Linages Legatos Jingled Jingles

80. Jolting Knights Logiest Ingates Ingesta Lankest Kinglet Ingoted

81. Inhaled Inhales Hostile Inflate Kindest Hotline Nailset Ladings

82. Ladinos Longish Longies Longest Kindles Indoles Lashing

83. Lasting Hosting Iodates Intakes Lathing Lofting Instead Khalifs

84. Ganoids Hokiest Hoisted Gelatin Genital Hoagies Hoidens

85. Histone Gelatos Hogtied Glinted Hogties Folates Folding

86. Foliage Honkies Foaling Foliate Folkies Folkish Fondest Holiest

87. Gahnite Holding Fondles Foisted Geoidal google Hasting

88. Hafting Hankies Handset Halides Handsel Haloids Haloing

89. Halting Heading Goatish Ghosted Hidalgo Gitanos Hefting

90. Halogen Glandes Glenoid Glisten Gloated Gnashed Heating

LESSON 4

KEYS ➤ Y , . (Period or full stop)

Note:

- To type symbol ".", bring down the **L** finger to the bottom row and type it.
- To type the letter "**y**", raise the **J** finger to the top row and type it.

1. y.ont .yont oy.nt yo.nt .oynt o.ynt n.yot .nyot yn.ot ny.ot .ynot

2. y.not yon.t oyn.t nyo.t yno.t ony.t noy.t no.yt on.yt .noyt n.oyt

3. o.nyt .onyt tony. otny. ntoy. tnoy. onty. noty. yotn. oytn. tyon.

4. yton. otyn. toyn. tnyo. ntyo. ytno. tyno. nyto. ynto. ynot. nyot.

5. oynt. yont. noyt. onyt. .nyto n.yto y.nto .ynto ny.to yn.to tn.yo

6. nt.yo .tnyo t.nyo n.tyo .ntyo .ytno y.tno t.yno .tyno yt.no ty.no

7. tyn.o ytn.o nty.o tny.o ynt.o nyt.o oyt.n yot.n toy.n oty.n yto.n

8. tyo.n .yotn y.otn o.ytn .oytn yo.tn oy.tn ot.yn to.yn .otyn o.tyn

9. t.oyn .toyn .tyon t.yon y.ton .yton ty.on yt.on nt.oy tn.oy .ntoy

10. n.toy t.noy .tnoy otn.y ton.y not.y ont.y tno.y nto.y n.oty .noty

11. on.ty no.ty .onty o.nty o.tny .otny to.ny ot.ny .tony t.ony Yet.

12. Yes. Yen. Nay. Hay. Jay. Say. Lay. Kay. Joy. Toy. Eye. Tea

13. Skylighted Thylakoids teasingly thylakoid steadying ankylosed

14. Dashingly daylights athelings defoliant deflation deflating.

15. Eightfold defiantly angelfish alongside desalting longheads.

16. Safelight legations fanlights Giltheads hailstone halftones.

17. Fashioned ghostlike flagstone gatefolds hosteling insolated.

18. Holytides hyalogens hayfields Holidays inflated holdings.

19. Holdfast hayfield insolate jokingly hidalgos headlong hedonist.

20. Jadishly isolated jostling headings Haylofts hyoidean holytide.

21. Halogens hyalites kinglets Hyalogen handiest hotlines hyaloids.

22. Handlist honestly hyalines lightens lankiest longhead lekythos.

23. Kyanites leadings neoliths ladyfish linkages Latigoes nylghais.

24. Knighted knightly sedating Sedation loathing leashing oafishly.

25. Loadings legation tangelos signaled sodality softhead slighted.

26. Skylight songlike toadfish sinkhole thionyls sodalite sneakily.

27. Shinleaf shingled steading Stonefly stodgily sidelong stealing.

28. Takingly stalking toadying toadyish toenails Shoaling steadily.

29. Skinhead shafting alighted diastole dotingly diagnose antilogy.

30. Elations atheling anolytes dystonia delaying ankylose delights.

31. Dealings ethinyls adhesion dayflies daylight Dealfish adjoints.

32. Delating deashing astonied Genitals goatfish feltings goldfish.

33. Foliaged goatskin fleshing fanglike gelatins good flighted.

34. Gelation fanlight floating fatlings finagled foliated flokatis.

35. Halftone gatefold flakiest gasoline gadflies gilthead feasting.

36. Finagles flashing flytings foliates yodeling yolkiest yeasting.

37. Staking Staying Slaking Stonily Shoeing Sleight Skyline.

38. Stained Thyself Stoking Tenfold Sighted Slinked Tasking.

39. Slaying Singled Thanked Stalked Slating Tangoed Tangles.

40. Singlet Slanged Teasing Tangelo Staling Skatole Thionyl.

41. Tangled Slanted Shaking Shakily Toenail Tingles Tingled.

42. Stygian Shanked Toadies Shafted Soilage Tinkles Shading.

43. Shadily Shadfly Tinkled Takings Staidly Stifled Talkies Talking.

44. Styling Shingle Shingly Shitake Shoaled Skating Soaking.

45. Snidely Synodal Styloid Shifted Isogeny Iodates Isolate.

46. Honesty Hoydens Isohyet Jangled Honkeys Jesting Jointed.

47. Jitneys Jingoes Jingles Jingled Hostile Hidalgo Hotline Hosting.

48. Honkies Jangles Hyaline Histone Hoisted Hokiest Inflate.

49. Hyaloid Holding Indoles Holiday Hyenoid Holiest Ingesta.

50. Hoidens Intakes Hoagies Instead Ingates Inhales Inhaled.

51. Hogtied Hogties Ingoted Hyalite Khalifs Kindest Healing.

52. Heating Handset Handsel Kindles Joshing Handles Kalends.

53. Heading Hayloft Kalongs Kidneys Headily Handily Hasting.

54. Jostled Keloids Haloing Kayoing Haloids Hankies Halogen.

55. Joisted Jointly Kinglet Heftily Hastily Halting Hefting Jolting.

56. Ligands Ligated Lashing Linages Lasting Ligates Lankest.

57. Lighten Neolith Onstage Nastily Olefins Lighted Leafing.

58. Leaking Nosegay Leasing Legions Nylghai Legatos Lengths.

59. Lengthy Leading Lathing Okaying Latigos Nightly Noyades.

60. Lentoid Lentigo Notedly Kyanite Ladinos Loathed Sandlot.

61. Ladings Loafing Leftish Loading Logiest Longish Longies.

62. Salting Kything Longest Sandhog Seating Loathes Nakedly.

63. Nailset Lingoes Sainted Lysogen Sealing Lofting Knights.

64. Saintly Salient Linkage Fetidly Gnashed Floated Goatish.

65. Flaking Felting Goalies Flagons Flokati Gloated Glisten Finagle

66. Gitanos Finales Flashed Flanked Flanges Flanged Geoidal.

67. Fishnet Ghostly Ghosted Flasket Genital Flaying.

68. Flinted Glinted Gelatin Fidgets Fidgety Flighty Flights Glenoid.

69. Gelatos Glandes Ghastly Folding Fogyish Faintly Folkies.

70. Fasting Folkish Foliate Fantods Hafting Foisted Falsity Fanjets.

71. Fainted Fanlike Foliage Fashion Gahnite Flyting Halides.

72. Foaling Folates Fondles Fatling Fondest Ganoids Fatlike.

73. Doeskin Dialogs Detains Details Anethol Dogfish Destiny.

74. Dingoes Dingles Alkynes Dingeys Disyoke Dilates Diglots.

75. Daylong Anolyte Deafish Defying Antilog Dealing Antlike.

76. Deathly Anklets Delight Dangles Dankest Defiant Dentils.

77. Dentals Density Densify Anisole Denials Dashing Defangs.

78. Doglike Eloigns Eoliths Dotages Easting Doylies Entails Elysian

79. Aiglets Enfolds Elating Etalons Ethanol Elastin Elation Doltish.

80. Alights Adenyls Aligned Agonies Donkeys Donates Ethinyl.

81. Elfish defats defang eloign dental deftly defogs enfold deaths.

82. Etalon dating enjoys dankly danios dangle ethnos eolith eolian.

83. Daylit deasil enhalo enlist enokis ethion entail deafly doings.

84. Dosing diglot digest dotage doting dialog doyens dhotis dholes.

85. Detain dilate dosage doling distal donate dongas dinghy.

86. Dingey dyeing detail delist eidola eights eighty eikons delfts.

87. Delays elands deking deltas denial egoist dynast easily design.

88. Easing desalt dentil eating edgily deigns alsike aligns alight.

89. Aliens algoid aldose aisled asking aiglet atoned anoles angels.

90. Angled alkyne alkyds alkies aliyot angles ankles anklet anodes.

91. Atones agents afield ageist adjoin dagoes adenyl aglets dainty.

92. Daftly agedly daikon keloid ketols hyoids keying ideals idlest.

CHAPTER 4

PRACTICE LESSONS 5 TO 8

IN THIS CHAPTER

▸▸ Lesson 5

  ▪ KEYS ➤ | , | , | W | , | R | , | B |

▸▸ Lesson 6

  ▪ KEYS ➤ | M | , | U | , | P | , | C |

▸▸ Lesson 7

  ▪ KEYS ➤ | V | , | X | , | Q | , | Z |

▸▸ Lesson 8

  KEYS ➤ ALL KEYS ➤ [Complete Sentences]

LESSON 5

KEYS ➤ , , W , R , B

Note:

- To type symbol ",", bring down the **K** finger to the bottom row and type it.
- To type the letter "**w**", raise the **S** finger to the top row and type it.
- To type the letter "**r**", raise the **F** finger to the top row and type it.
- To type the letter "**b**", bring down the **F** finger to the bottom row and type it.

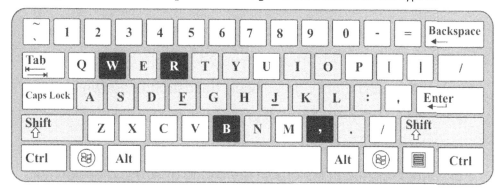

1. ,,, ,,w ,,r ,,b ,w, ,ww ,wr ,wb ,r, ,rw ,rr ,rb ,b, ,bw ,br ,bb w,, w,w

2. w,r w,b ww, www wwr wwb wr, wrw wrr wrb wb, wbw wbr wbb r,,

3. r,w r,r r,b rw, rww rwr rwb rr, rrw rrr rrb rb, rbw rbr rbb b,, b,w b,r

4. b,b bw, bww bwr bwb br, brw brr brb bb, bbw bbr bbb ,r,b,r,b, ,,b

5. yyy yy. yyn yy, yyw yyr yyb y.y y.. y.n y., y.w y.r y.b yny yn. ynn

6. yn, ynw ynr ynb y,y y,. y,n y,, y,w y,r y,b ywy yw. ywn yw, yww ,,

7. ywr ywb yry yr. yrn yr, yrw yrr yrb yby yb. ybn yb, ybw ybr ybb .yy

8. .y. .yn .y, .yw .yr .yb ..y ... ..n .., ..w ..r ..b .ny .n. .nn .n, .nw .nr .,,.

9. .nb .,y .,. .,n .,, .,w .,r .,b .wy .w. .wn .w, .ww .wr .wb .ry .r. .rn .r, .,

10. .rw .rr .rb .by .b. .bn .b, .bw .br .bb nyy ny. nyn ny, nyw nyr nyb.

11. n,, n,w n,r n,b nwy nw. nwn nw, nww nwr nwb nry nr. nrn nr, nrw,

12. nrr nrb nby nb. nbn nb, nbw nbr nbb ,yy ,y. ,yn ,y, ,yw ,yr ,yb ,.y,

13. ,.. ,.n ,., ,.w ,.r ,.b ,ny ,n. ,nn ,n, ,nw ,nr ,nb ,,y ,,. ,,n ,,, ,,w ,,r ,,b,

14. ,wy ,w. ,wn ,w, ,ww ,wr ,wb ,ry ,r. ,rn ,r, ,rw ,rr ,rb ,by ,b. ,bn ,b, r,

15. ,bw ,br ,bb wyy wy. wyn wy, wyw wyr wyb w.y w.. w.n w., w.w w.r

16. w.b wny wn. wnn wn, wnw wnr wnb w,y w,. w,n w,, w,w w,r w,b r,

17. wwy ww. wwn ww, www wwr wwb wry wr. wrn wr, wrw wrr wrb w

18. wby wb. wbn wb, wbw wbr wbb ryy ry. ryn ry, ryw ryr ryb r.y r.. r,

19. rwy rw. rwn rw, rww rwr rwb rry rr. rrn rr, rrw rrr rrb rby rb. rbn rb,

20. rbw rbr rbb byy by. byn by, byw byr byb b.y b.. b.n b., b.w b.r b.b

21. bny bn. bnn bn, bnw bnr bnb b,y b,. b,n b,, b,w b,r b,b bwy bw. w

22. bwn bw, bww bwr bwb bry br. brn br, brw brr brb bby bb. bbn bb,

23. Designatory downrightly grandiosely headstrong handwrites

24. handiworks blathering batfowling blandisher Bandoliers

25. anhydrites anglerfish arytenoids afterglows fieldworks beer

26. Farsighted flybridges fingerhold defrosting destroying designator

27. Drinkables defoliants desolating dwarfishly deflations earthlings

28. Forestland freakishly girandoles flyweights folksinger fosterling

29. Dayflowers boyfriends breakdowns breathings debonairly

30. Deathblows bolstering labyrinths kohlrabies ladyfinger lakefronts

31. Hydrations interfolds holstering obeisantly refloating worktables

32. Windbreaks shrinkable shadowlike lobstering longhaired

33. Neighborly lengthways slathering stewarding skylighted

34. Thylakoids toweringly threadfins threading threadfin teardowns

35. Teasingly swordtail thinkable tailbones thinkably thylakoid

36. Thyroidal tarnished tangibles takedowns wreathing yearlings

37. Wristband wrestling wolfsbane windbreak windblast worktable

38. Hosteling hyalogens horsetail horntails ingathers insolated

39. Hoardings interlays integrals ingrowths interflow interfold

40. Jargonish ingrafted ignorable hydrolase inflators idolaters

41. Hydration hydrating hobnailed hydrogels hydrogens holytides

42. Weaklings wearingly treadling triangles waterlogs waterdogs

43. Troweling twanglers lathering kingbolts lakefront koshering

44. Lawyering kilobytes keyboards kyboshing karyotins labyrinth

45. Laborites reloading refolding ordinates refashion restyling

46. Restoking obligated reobtains reflating organdies regionals

47. Reshowing reflowing reflation rebodying relations obligates

48. Obtainers streaking signboard soldering strangled snakebird

49. Strangely steadying signatory snowdrift snowflake steroidal

50. Strobilae snowfield sangfroid safelight shakedown ringbolts

51. Shadowing showbread showering shearling royalties seaworthy

52. Rewashing shrinkage rhyolites leadworks legations longhairs

53. Narghiles lifeworks lifeboats nightjars longheads legionary

54. Neighbors deathblow breathily dawsonite breathing breasting

55. Breakdown brawliest dashingly boneyards dayflower brawniest

56. Daylights debarking bystander bothering daneworts bowstring

57. Defiantly boyfriend breakings brightens anhydrite alongside

58. Abolished abolisher afterglow adoringly arytenoid adsorbing

59. Angelfish astringed aeroliths ankylosed bandolier athelings

60. Adsorbent banderols handworks gradients hairstyle hayfields

61. Halftones hangbirds haltering handiwork goatherds handwrote

62. Handwrite hailstone headfirst headworks herbalist heralding

63. Globefish grandiose gyrations bigotedly beadworks beholding

64. Batfowled baritones bestowing bearishly blowhards biathlons

65. Barytones bastioned betraying blighters bewraying birthdays

66. Biosafety frontages foresight foresting ghastlier fostering

67. Gatefolds giltheads girandole garnished forehands geraniols

68. Forelands gasholder forewings frightens gearshift flyweight

69. Ghostlier forsythia forsaking frangible gawkishly ghostlike

70. Flowering fieldwork flatirons fashioned flatworks finaglers

71. Fleaworts firsthand floriated fireboats florigens flagstone faltering

72. Falsework fashioner fathering estradiol fanlights flybridge

73. Farthings downshift dwarflike downbeats downstage downright

74. Desorbing desirably dragonish dragonets drawknife drawliest

75. Desalting drinkable dragonfly draglines earthling defraying

76. Dishwater defoliant eightfold definably deflators dishtowel

77. Doweling downbeat diablery detrains downiest diagnose

78. Dogbanes dishware dorkiest deorbits delights delating elations

79. Dwarfing driblets deflator drawling driftage deniably drystone

80. Drawings drowsily drowsing hibernal goldfish handiest google

81. Growable gradient grosbeak greasily grayfish granites hairnets

82. Handwork hayrides haywires headwork headlong hearting

83. Hedonist heartily bowheads boneyard bowering danewort

84. Brothels darlings danglers brigands bristled dayworks breaking

85. Dealfish brighten bodhrans debasing daylight brigades dayflies

86. Broadens bondages broadest breading brawnily ailerons

87. Antilogy adhesion adhering ankylose bankside alienors atheling

88. Bankerly abridges asteroid banished absinthe balkiest absently

89. Althorns banisher banister filberts flingers farinose firedogs

90. Flatbeds flashing flashier fanlight fishable blinkers blowhard

LESSON 6

KEYS ➤ M , U , P , C

Note:

- To type the letter "**m**", bring down the **J** finger to the bottom row and type it.
- To type the letter "**u**", raise the **J** finger to the top row and type it.
- To type the letter "**p**", raise the **;** finger to the top row and type it.
- To type the letter "**c**", bring down the **D** finger to the bottom row and type it.

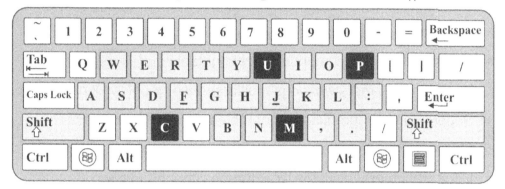

1. m m m m m u m m p m m c m u m m u u m u p m u c m p

2. m m p u m p p m p c m cm m cu m cp m cc u m m u m u u

3. m p u m c u u m u u u u u p u u c u p m u p u u p p u p c u

4. cm u cu u cp u cc p m m p m u p m p p m c p u m p u u p

5. u p p u c p p m p p u p p p p p c p cm p cu p cp p cc cm m

6. cm u cm p cm c cu m cu u cu p cu c cp m cp u cp p cp cb

7. Wm m Wm u Wm p Wm c Wm W Wm R Wm B Wu m Wu u

8. Wu p Wu c Wu W Wu R Wu B Wp m Wp u Wp p Wp c Wp c

9. W Wp R Wp B Wcm Wcu Wcp Wcc WcW WcR WcB WWm c

10. WWu WWp WWc WWW WWR WWB WRm WRu WRp bc b

11. WRc WRW WRR WRB WBm WBu WBp WBc WBW WBR cc

12. WBB Rm m Rm u Rm p Rm c Rm W Rm R Rm B Ru m Ru u

13. Ru p Ru c Ru W Ru R Ru B Rp m Rp u Rp p Rp c Rp W Rp

14. R Rp B Rcm Rcu Rcp Rcc RcW RcR RcB RWm RWu RWp

15. RWc RWW RWR RWB RRm RRu RRp RRc RRW RRR RRB

16. RBm RBu RBp RBc RBW RBR RBB Bm m Bm u Bm p Bm

17. c Bm W Bm R Bm B Bu m Bu u Bu p Bu c Bu W Bu R Bu B

18. Bp m Bp u Bp p Bp c Bp W Bp R Bp B Bcm Bcu Bcp Bccc

19. BcW BcR BcB BWm BWu BWp BWc BWW BWR BWB BRm

20. BRu BRp BRc BRW BRR BRB BBm BBu BBp BBc BBW cc

21. Dermatoglyphics uncopyrightable troublemakings

22. Dermatoglyphic documentarily copyrightable hydromagnetic

23. Lycanthropies metalworkings multibranched troublemaking

24. Subordinately unpredictably unproblematic endolymphatic

25. Flowchartings flowcharting farsightedly euchromatins

26. Edulcorating granulocytes lycanthropes imponderably

27. Incomputable housewarming malnourished bluestocking.

28. Bankruptcies cabinetworks considerably demographics.

29. Demonstrably discountable discrepantly disreputably.

30. Upholstering unprofitable unprofitably stickhandler stenograph

31. Thunderclaps problematics multipronged metalworking.

32. Mendaciously packinghouse outspreading nightwalkers.

33. Pelargoniums polycentrism playgrounds pitchforked playwright

34. Polyandries mindblowers meroblastic microphages misanthrop

35. Misanthrope outdreaming outmarching outcharming.

36. Myelopathic mustachioed multiagency motherlands.

37. Phlebograms percolating peculations personality pelargonium.

38. Phantomlike patronymics parbuckling outreaching palindromes.

39. Pathfinders neuropathic neutrophils nefariously nightwalker.

40. Obfuscating campgrounds cabinetwork amblygonite.

41. Atmospheric archegonium amylopectin birthplaces blackthorns.

42. Bichromates abolishment abridgments achondrites.

43. Backgrounds backlighted beachfronts badmouthing.

44. Blameworthy bodysurfing blaspheming grandiosely granulocyte

45. Groupthinks goldfinches fluoridates foremanship floribundas.

46. Forecasting fluorinates flyspecking fluorescing fluorinated.

47. Fractiously furbelowing formulating glucosamine geophysical.

48. Glucokinase glauconites genotypical embracingly endoplasmic

49. Factorylike facetiously elucidators euphoriants euchromatin.

50. Fingerholds filamentous filmography fisherwoman feldspathic.

51. Hectoringly macrophytes importunely inculpatory inscrutable.

52. Hypogastric inosculated hypsometric hypokalemic impregnably

53. Imprudently inscrutably hypodermics lumberjacks lowercasing.

54. Lycanthrope lymphokines lawrenciums ligamentous huckster

55. Hydroplanes intercampus insuperably keyboardist keyboarding.

56. Lactiferous ladyfingers kymographic prosecuting predictably.

57. Profligates precautions problematic preachingly promulgated.

58. Pratincoles postmarking predynastic proselyting prognathism.

59. Promulgates readjusting punchboards pyromancies radiolucent

60. Righteously roundtables screamingly secondarily searchingly.

61. Semaphoring scenography republicans recomputing.

62. Regulations reductional shouldering speculating spaceflight.

63. Speculation duplicators dragonflies doublethink dumbwaiters.

64. Downrightly drumbeating confirmedly complainers countryfied.

65. Countryside countrywide conjugality conjugately construable.

66. Confirmable copyrighted comradeship counterbids copyreading

67. Compatibles craftswomen customarily clergywoman.

68. Chrysomelid clofibrates centrifugal chlorinated chlorinates.

69. Chloramines charmingest delusionary demographic.

70. Dangerously designatory documentary discography disgraceful

71. Disturbance thunderclap tenaciously tambourines unseaworthy.

72. Unscrambled undesirably tragicomedy timberlands trampolines

73. Tourmalines wolframites workmanship ulcerations ultrafiches.

74. Superfamily subterminal subtropical switchboard switchblade.

75. Subordinate subcategory sulfonamide stenography strikebound

76. Stickhandle sporulating spirochetal warehousing waitperson.

77. Urogenital wainscoted wanderlust waterbucks upthrowing.

78. Wardenship womanliest worktables womanishly windbreaks.

79. Worshipful wolframite workplaces wingspread unsociably.

80. Unworkable underplays unchastely underplots unsteadily.

81. Unpolished unworthily unsociable ungodliest undercoats.

82. Unscripted untowardly upholstery unemphatic unscramble.

83. Undogmatic unshackled tambourine throwbacks thylakoids.

84. Thimerosal thumbnails thornbacks tambouring threadfins.

85. Theurgical thumbscrew trampoline toweringly tourmaline.

86. Touchlines timberland touchingly trialogues sporangium.

87. Stockinged stewarding stampeding sprightful stomaching.

88. Splotching stupefying springhead sporulated sportingly.

89. Stockpiled stepfamily ulceration ulcerating unactorish.

90. Truckloads ultrafiche ultrasonic tumbledown suboptimal.

91. Supertonic superwoman subtrahend supergiant switchable.

92. Subkingdom subrogated sublimated subjecting superlight.

93. Subnetwork subproject submarined superblock subheading.

94. Subcentral sulfonated syncopated sulphating subdialect.

95. Subjection surjection subchapter switchyard syndicator.

96. Headspring hermatypic handwrites headstrong handsomely.

97. Hectograms handiworks fosterling fractioned fortalices.

98. Freakishly fumigators fulminated fulminates fruitcakes.

99. Fornicated formulated franchised formulates graphemics.

100. Gyroplanes gyrfalcons gynarchies gramineous graciously.

101. Groupthink greyhounds grubstaked groundfish graticules.

102. Grouchiest flybridges fluoridate flamingoes fluorinate forestland

103. Floribunda flounciest flustering formidably formidable flyweights

104. Flowcharts flourished folksinger fancyworks fishmonger.

105. Fingerhold fingerpost fetchingly fieldworks farsighted falconries.

106. Goldbricks gluconates girandoles glutamines gelatinous.

107. Glycosuria goatsucker godparents gardenfuls godfathers.

108. Glauconite euphoriant elucidator eurybathic factiously.

109. Endophytic educations eukaryotic euphorbias factorship.

110. Epistolary emulations eurythmics nucleators neoplastic.

111. Obduracies neighborly obeisantly noticeably nebulosity.

112. Objurgates obfuscated objurgated narcolepsy nightclubs.

113. Neutrophil neutralism normalcies obdurately neuropathy.

114. Nightmares outlawries orbiculate outbarking outlandish.

115. Outlanders outflanked outcharmed outbeaming outclimbed.

116. Osculating outmarched outmarches outdrawing polyanthus

LESSON 7

KEYS ➤ V , X , Q , Z

Note:

- To type the letter "**v**", bring down the **F** finger to the bottom row and type it.
- To type the letter "**x**", bring down the **S** finger to the bottom row and type it.
- To type the letter "**q**", raise the **A** finger to the top row and type it.
- To type the letter "**z**", bring down the **A** finger to the bottom row and type it.

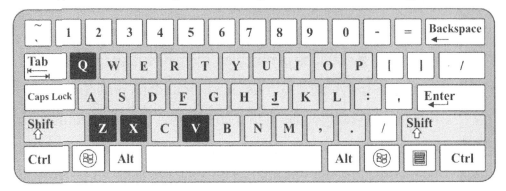

1. v v v v v v v x v v v q v v v z v v x v v v x x v v x q v v x z v v
2. qv v v qx v v qq v v qz v v zv v v zx v v zq v v zz v x v v v x v
3. x v x v q v x v z v x x v v x x x v x x q v x x z v x qv v x qx v x
4. qq v x qz v x zv v x zx v x zq v x zz v qv v v qv x v qv q v qv z
5. v qx v v qx x v qx q v qx z v qqv v qqx v qqq v qqz v qzv v
6. qzx v qzq v qzz v zv v v zv x v zv q v zv z v zx v v zx x v zx
7. q v zx z v zqv v zqx v zqq v zqz v zzv v zzx v zzq v zzz x v v
8. v x v v x x v v q x v v z x v x v x v x x x v x q x v x z x v qv x
9. v qx x v qq x v qz x v zv x v zx x v zq x v zz x x v v x x v x x
10. x v q x x v z x x x v x x x x x x x q x x x z x x qv x x qx x x qq
11. x x qz x x zv x x zx x x zq x x zz x qv v x qv x x qv q x qv z x
12. qx v x qx x x qx q x qx z x qqv x qqx x qqq x qqz x qzv x qzx
13. x qzq x qzz x zv v x zv x x zv q x zv z x zx v x zx x x zx q x zx
14. z x zqv x zqx x zqq x zqz x zzv x zzx x zzq x zzz qv v v qv v
15. x qv v q qv v z qv x v qv x x qv x q qv x z qv qv qv qx qv qq
16. qv qz qv zv qv zx qv zq qv zz qx v v qx v x qx v q qx v z qx x

17. v qx x x qx x q qx x z qx qv qx qx qx qq qx qz qx zv qx zx

18. qx zq qx zz qqv v qqv x qqv q qqv z qqx v qqx x qqx q qqx z

19. qqqv qqqx qqqq qqqz qqzv qqzx qqzq qqzz qzv v qzv x qzv

20. q qzv z qzx v qzx x qzx q qzx z qzqv qzqx qzqq qzqz qzzv

21. Evzones Evzone Exquisitenesses Exquisiteness Exquisitely

22. Zoogeographers Zombifications Zoogeographies Zombification

23. Exquisites Exquisite Zoogeographically Zoogeographical

24. Zooxanthellae Zoogeographer Zooplanktonic Zoogeographic

25. Zoosporangium Zoogeography Zoantharians Zooxanthella

26. Zoosporangia Zillionaires Zooplanktons Zooplankters

27. Zootechnical Zoologically Zwitterionic Zooplankter Zestfulness

28. Zootechnics Zooplankton Zealousness Zwitterions Zabagliones

29. Zillionaire Zoantharian Zidovudines Zemindaries Zygomorphic

30. Zookeepers Zoophilous Zinfandels Zincifying Zeitgeists

31. Zigzagging Zeitgebers Zoomorphic Zitherists Zebrawoods

32. Zoological Zombielike Zidovudine Zombifying Zealotries

33. Zoologists Zwitterion Zygodactyl Zygomorphy Zygosities

34. Zamindaris Zygospores Zucchettos Zabaglione Zebrawood

35. Zedoaries Zoochores Zinfandel Zwiebacks Zincified Zebrasses

36. Zucchinis Zincifies Zamindari Zestfully Zymograms Zonetimes

37. Zitherist Zeppelins Zippering Zirconium Zemindary Zombified

38. Zombifies Zeitgeist Zygomatic Zymogenes Zigzagged

39. Zarzuelas Zygospore Zoophilic Zoosterol Ziggurats Zaratites

40. Zoophobes Zoophytes Zeitgeber Zoospores Zoosperms

41. Zoophiles Zealously Zillionth Zymurgies Zoolaters Zucchetto

42. Zamindars Zoologies Zoologist Zookeeper Zippiest Zymosans

43. Ziggurat Zirconia Zincates Zillions Zingiest Zincking Zoisites

44. Zincites Zymology Zyzzyvas Zymogram Zippered Zymogens

45. Zoolater Zoolatry Zorilles Zoologic Zootomic Zoomania

46. Zoometry Zoonoses Zoonosis Zoophobe Zoophyte Zoospore

47. Zymogene Zodiacal Zygotene Zonetime Zygosity Zonation

48. Zoonotic Zoochore Zooecium Zoogenic Zwieback Zucchini

49. Zoosperm Zestiest Zarzuela Zaratite Zaptiehs Zappiest

50. Zaibatsu Zapateos Zaniness Zemstvos Zelkovas Zeppelin
51. Vasoconstrictions Vasoconstrictive Vasoconstriction
52. Zecchins Zealotry Zibeline Zamindar Zenithal Zeolitic Zeolites
53. Vasoconstrictors Videoconferences Xeroradiography
54. Zestless Videoconferencing Valetudinarianism
55. Xerographically Xenophobically Xerophthalmias Xerophthalmia
56. Quantificationally Quattuordecillions Quattuordecillion
57. Xenodiagnoses Xylographical Xerophthalmic Xanthophylls
58. Quatercentenaries Quarterfinalists Quantificational
59. Xylophonists Xylographers Xylographic Xenobiotics Xerophilies
60. Quadruplications Quadricentennial Quintessentially
61. Xylophagous Xerophilous Xerothermic Xylographer
62. Quintuplicating Quatercentenary Quarterfinalist
63. Xerographic Xerophytism Xylophonist Xanthophyll
64. Quarrelsomeness Quadruplicities Quantifications
65. Aardvark Ablative Abortive Abrasive Absolved Absolver
66. Quadruplicating Quadruplication Quarterbacking Quantitatively
67. Absolves Achieved Achiever Achieves Activate Actively
68. Qualifications Quantification Quadrillionths Quartermasters
69. Activism Activist Activity Adaptive Additive Adhesive Adjuvant
70. Quadrilaterals Quasiparticles Quinquennially Quadrumvirates
71. Adoptive Advanced Advancer Advances Advected Adverted
72. Quadruplicates Quadruplicated Quindecillions Questionnaires
73. Advisees Advisers Advising Advisors Advisory Advocacy
74. Quintuplicates Quintessential Quintuplicated Quintillionths
75. Advocate Advowson Agentive Aggrieve Airwaves Akvavits
76. Bedevils Beehives Behalves Behavers Behaving Behavior
77. Alewives Allovers Allusive Alluvial Alluvion Alluvium Alveolar
78. Behooved Behooves Believed Believer Believes Beloveds
79. Alveolus Ambivert Approval Approved Approver Approves
80. Cadavers Calvados Calvaria Canvased Canvases Captives
81. Aquavits Archival Archived Archives Arrivals Arrivers Arriving
82. Bereaved Bereaves Bevatron Beveling Beveller Beverage

83. Atavisms Atavists Auditive Avadavat Availing Avarices Avellane
84. Bevomits Biconvex Biovular Bivalent Bivalves Bivouacs
85. Avengers Avenging Aventail Averaged Averages Averment
86. Bloviate Bolivars Bovinely Bovinity Bravados Breveted Breviary
87. Avocados Avoiders Avoiding Avouched Avouches Avowable
88. Caravans Caravels Carnival Carvings Cassavas Cavalier
89. Averring Aversely Aversion Aversive Averting Aviaries Aviating
90. Cavallas Cavatina Caveated Cavefish Caverned Cavettos
91. Aviation Aviators Aviatrix Avidness Avifauna Avionics
92. Cavicorn Cavilers Caviling Cavitary Cavitate Cavitied Cavities
93. Avowedly Avulsing Avulsion Baklavas Beavered Bedcover
94. Cavorted Cavorter Centavos Cervelat Cervical Cervices
95. Deceived Deceiver Deceives Decemvir Decisive Decurved
96. Cervixes Chervils Cheviots Chevrons Chivalry Chivaree
97. Chivvied Chivvies Chivying Civilian Civility Civilize Clavicle
98. Devising Devisors Devoiced Devoices Devolved Devolves
99. Devotees Devoting Devotion Devoured Devourer Devoutly
100. Claviers Cleavage Cleavers Cleaving Cleveite Cleverer
101. Coevally Coevolve Cognovit Cohesive Coinvent Commoved
102. Cleverly Clevises Coactive Codriver Codrives Coercive
103. Dilative Dilutive Diluvial Diluvian Diluvium Disavows Discover
104. Commoves Conative Concaved Concaves Conceive Conclave
105. Disfavor Dishevel Disprove Dissaved Dissaves Disserve
106. Convexly Conveyed Conveyer Conveyor Convicts Convince
107. Cordovan Corrival Corvette Corvinas Covalent Covenant
108. Dissever Dissolve Disvalue Divagate Divalent Divebomb
109. Coverage Coverall Coverers Covering Coverlet Coverlid
110. Diverged Diverges Diverted Diverter Divested Dividend
111. Covertly Coverups Coveters Coveting Covetous Cravenly
112. Dividers Dividing Divinely Diviners Divinest Divining Divinity
113. Cravings Creative Crescive Crevalle Crevasse Creviced
114. Divinize Division Divisive Divisors Divorced Divorcee Divorcer
115. Crevices Cultivar Culverin Culverts Curative Cursives Curvedly

LESSON 8

ALL KEYS ➤ [Complete Sentences]

Note:

- Type only the text, do not type the line number shown in the gray color.
- Use **Backspace** or **Delete** key to correct a mistyped word.
- When a line ends, press **Enter** key using the right little finger.

1.   We clearly, cannot stop natural hazards from happening.

2.   An old man had a fall and banged his head hard.

3.   My best friend has been a companion to me.

4.   Call the computer company to cancel collection.

5.   Buy a ball for Beth and bring it back in a bag.

6.   Handicraft work is practiced mostly by women in the world.

7.   Every evening after tea he went to see Georgie.

8.   Did I decorate the dining room in December.

9.   If you don't conquer your fears, they will beat you.

10. The good guy in the story was strong and kind.

11. There are eight paragraphs in this essay.

12. It was really dark, and I couldn't see anything

13. A person needs to see his dentist twice a year.

14. Palwasha runs with her dog on Sundays.

15. Evening is to morning as dinner is to breakfast.

16. Butcher is to knife as a hairdresser is to scissors.

17. Warm is to hot as old is to oldest.

18. My sister and I were at my grandma's house.

19. Working late into the night, Umar fell asleep on his desk.

20. Get a good grip on the gate, and drag it along.

21. Fill a fat frog with food from the first floor.

22. Have a happy holiday at Hastings Hall in March.

23. I will fill it with a lining first to insulate.

24. Just ask Jane to judge the jitterbug and tango.

25. The kind king gave back a kettle to the tinker.

26. No new newspapers need to be sent to Ned today.

27. Adora lost her silver locket at Looe last year.

28. Some men made a magnificent machine from metal.

29. Please pack the pots into paper packs promptly.

30. Clive opted to organize the food on the outing.

31. Ronald ran a race to raise revenue for charity.

32. Show us some seashells and shiny silver stars.

33. Queenie requested varied questions in the quiz.

34. The extra anxious taxi man was extremely vexed.

35. A bee buzzed lazily as it zoomed round the zoo.

36. They say they should pay for the toy by cheque.

37. We got wet when we went walking near the woods.

38. The undergraduate undertook to shut up the box.

39. Very enviable views were seen in the village.

40. The toy teddy was fixed to the top of the tree.

41. We had reached home before the sunset

42. Necessity is a mother of invention.

43. Nothing comes amiss to a hungry man

44. There is a large Rain Forest in South America.

45. He knocked several times, no one came to the door.

46. He turned in the exploration paper on Friday; else, he would have not passed the class.

47. She exhorted him to return without a moment's delay.

48. Inquire tomorrow; I will check whether the book has arrived.

49. I checked to ensure that he was as yet alive.

50. The stream stole the divine beings.

51. A sparkling jewel isn't enough.

52. She generally addresses him in a boisterous voice.

53. The outsider administers the supper.

54. He came up short on cash, so he needed to quit playing poker.

55. I need more nitty gritty data.

56. John made the sugar treats; Fudan brightened them.

57. She did her best to encourage him.

58. He disclosed to us an extremely energizing experience story.

59. The speedy dark colored fox hops over the apathetic puppy.

60. Mary plays the piano.

61. She just paints with striking hues; she doesn't care for pastels.

62. She didn't undermine the test, for it was not the best activity.

63. Sixty-Four comes requesting bread.

64. We must lease a space for our gathering.

65. Give me a chance to assist you with your stuff.

66. Tom got a little bit of pie.

67. Try not to venture on the broken glass.

68. Shake music approaches at high speed.

69. I figure I will purchase the red auto, or I will rent the blue one.

70. She generally addresses him in a boisterous voice.

71. Stunning, does that work?

72. It was getting dim, and we weren't there yet.

73. The old apple delights in its position.

74. Try not to venture on the broken glass.

75. I hear that Nancy is lovely.

76. He came up short on cash, so he needed to quit playing poker.

77. He revealed to us an exceptionally energizing experience story.

78. Kindly hold up outside of the house.

79. The shooter says farewell to his affection.

80. Students accede to their teacher's proposal.

81. They should not exceed the limits.

82. Jahan accepted my offer.

83. All danced in the party except Ahmad.

84. Those adapt to new environment are the successful people.

85. Kamran is supposed to be adept in computer literacy.

86. Professor Malik adopts the research of his seniors.

87. Students love to love addition questions.

88. This third edition of the book published in 1980.

89. The adverse weather conditions made us late.

90. The poet and critic Shadab are averse to criticism.

More Sentences

Note:

- Type only the text, do not type the line number shown in the gray color.
- Use **Backspace** or **Delete** key to correct a mistyped word.
- When a line ends, press **Enter** key using right little finger.

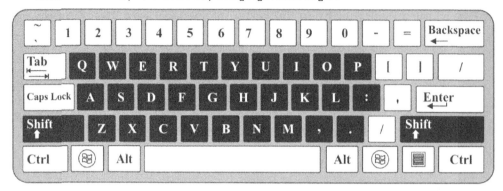

1. The teacher advised his class on the day of his retirement.

2. His calm words affected more than lectures his poor conduct.

3. I see an effect of this book on the behavior of students.

4. He reads the book aloud.

5. The principal allowed his teacher to remain on casual leave.

6. William stood silent in front of the altar for five minutes.

7. Shabnam alters her scarf back to front.

8. The children had already left the hostel when we reached.

9. We are **all** ready to depart.

10. The teacher alluded again and again to his new plan.

11. The mice eluded the trap.

12. The audience understood the allusion of the speaker.

13. His arguments were nothing but illusion.

14. The students in terms of behavior declared amoral.

15. Modern societies never welcome immoral behavior.

16. On the annual gathering, our school had a grand party.

17. The documents proved the agreement annulled.

18. We shall appraise the situation.

19. The students were apprised of their results.

20. After climbing the ascent, we were dead tired.

21. The agreement is settled after their assent.

22. I assure you that you will win.

23. The company assures you that product will not break.

24. The carpenter puts these holes with an auger.

25. The professors of physics augur a minor collision.

26. I warned them not to run bare footed.

27. The students bear school dues.

28. My father reserved a berth in the rail way.

29. Peshawar is my birth place.

30. We live beside the canal road.

31. The holiday trip was besides all the other basic facilities.

32. She has blonde highlights in her hair.

33. James is the only blond in our school.

34. He was born Abbottabad.

35. This car is air borne.

36. We bought a new house.

37. We brought the furniture home in a truck.

38. The driver applied brakes to stop the vehicle

39. She breaks the cup by a mistake.

40. The girl brought herself a bridal dress.

41.   The coach driver drew the bridles.

42.   The wrestling ring is covered with canvas.

43.   This cereal is for children.

44.   We loved to watch "Dhua" drama serial.

45.   We bought coarse cloth for dishing.

46.   The students were taught the course in time.

47.   The applause of the audience was a great compliment.

48.   It is efforts worked towards the complement of the scheme.

49.   He attended the meeting continually.

50.   It was raining continuously for three days.

51.   The credible reputation is everything.

52.   His achievements are creditable.

53.   The rulers know how to curb an adverse situation.

54.   The pedestrians avoid walking on the kerb.

55.   I love to eat currant.

56.   We cannot swim against the current of a river.

57.   Arab is a desert country.

58.   The guests were served with dessert after the meal.

59.   This is the original device.

60.   The workers devised a plan which provided them relief.

61.   His good manners announced him a discreet figure.

62.   This figure has discrete value.

63.   His first draft was more than a success.

64.   The draught made the room cool.

65.   The elicited documents are mostly reliable.

66. Government takes notice of illicit construction these days.

67. His success was imminent on the grounds of his hard work.

68. Despite his best effort, he could not free himself.

69. A few days later, the lion was caught in a hunter's trap.

70. Even a little creature maybe of a great help.

71. But he was too impatient to wait for several months.

72. They began to dance with joy, as soon as they heard that.

73. He who digs a pit for others, himself falls into it.

74. The project was planned by joining small pieces of land.

75. Students became workers of different political parties.

76. Ultimately, their investment was kicked badly affected.

77. Independence of the judiciary was guaranteed.

78. All the people are equal in the eyes of law.

79. Free radical is represented by a dot over the symbol.

80. As atoms are extremely small particles and are invisible.

81. Compound is a substance made up of two or more elements.

82. A problem is an obstacle, difficulty or challenge.

83. Determine whether a given number is prime number or not.

84. The floods badly affected the people and environment.

85. The windows of the hotel are beautifully constructed.

86. Who is a right writer to write a right note about the rights of right-hand driver?

87. He picked up a potato to smash it for baking.

88. One of the biggest effects of air pollution is global warming.

CHAPTER 5

PRACTICE LESSONS 8 TO 12

LESSON 9

KEYS ➤ 1 , 3 , 4 , 5 , 6 , 7 , 8 , 9 , 0

Note:

- Type numbers **1** to **5** with left hand and **6** to **0** with right hand.
- Remember the left **index** finger is responsible for numbers **4** and **5** and the right **index** finger for numbers **6** and **7**.

1.	0000 0001 0002 0003 0004 0005 0006 0007 0008 0009 000
2.	0010 0011 0012 0013 0014 0015 0016 0017 0018 0019 001
3.	0020 0021 0022 0023 0024 0025 0026 0027 0028 0029 002
4.	0030 0031 0032 0033 0034 0035 0036 0037 0038 0039 003
5.	0040 0041 0042 0043 0044 0045 0046 0047 0048 0049 004
6.	0050 0051 0052 0053 0054 0055 0056 0057 0058 0059 005
7.	0060 0061 0062 0063 0064 0065 0066 0067 0068 0069 006
8.	0070 0071 0072 0073 0074 0075 0076 0077 0078 0079 007
9.	0080 0081 0082 0083 0084 0085 0086 0087 0088 0089 008
10.	0090 0091 0092 0093 0094 0095 0096 0097 0098 0099 009
11.	Open123 lotus123 word2016 84613 00001 00012 00345 00023
12.	100 10as 10df 10gh 10 1as1 1as2 1as3 1as4 1as5 1as6 1as7
13.	1as8 1as9 1as0 1gh0 1ghas 1ghdf 1ghgh 1gh 11 12 13 14 15

14. 16 17 18 19 10 1as 1df 1gh 1 2asas 2asdf 2asgh 2as 2df1 2df2

15. 2df3 2df4 2df5 2df6 2df7 2df8 2df9 2df0 35df 35gh 35 361 362

16. 363 364 365 366 367 368 369 360 36as 36df 36gh 36 4asas

17. 4asdf 4asgh 4as 4df1 4df2 4df3 4df4 4df5 4df6 4df7 4df8 4df9

18. 4df0 4dfas 4dfdf 4dfgh 4df 4gh1 4gh2 4gh3 4gh4 4gh5 4gh6

19. 4gh7 4gh8 4gh9 5asas 5asdf 5asgh 5as 5df1 5df2 5df3 5df4

20. 5df5 5df6 5df7 5df8 5df9 5df0 640 64as 64df 64gh 64 651 652

21. 653 654 655 656 657 658 659 650 65as 6gh0 6ghas 6ghdf

22. 6ghgh 6gh 61 62 63 64 65 66 67 68 69 60 6as 6df 6gh 6 7asas

23. 7asdf 7asgh 7as 7df1 7df2 7df3 7df4 7df5 7df6 7df7 7df8 7df9

24. 7df0 8dfas 8dfdf 8dfgh 8df 8gh1 8gh2 8gh3 8gh4 8gh5 8gh6

25. 8gh7 8gh8 8gh9 911 912 913 914 915 916 917 918 919 910

26. 91as 91df 91gh 91 921 922 923 924 938 939 930 93as 93df

27. 96gh 96 971 972 973 974 975 976 977 978 979 970 97as 97df

28. 97gh 97 981 982 983 984 985 986 987 988 989 980 98as 98df

29. 98gh 98 991 992 993 994 995 996 997 998 999 990 99as 99df

30. 99gh 99 901 902 903 904 905 906 907 908 909 900 90as 90df

31. 90gh 90 9as1 9as2 9as3 9as4 9as5 9as6 9as7 9as8 9as9 9as0

32. 9asas 9asdf 9asgh 9as 9df1 9df2 9df3 9df4 9df5 9df6 9df7 9df8

33. 9df9 9df0 9dfas 9dfdf 9dfgh 9df 9gh1 9gh2 9gh3 9gh4 9gh5

34. 9gh6 9gh7 9gh8 9gh9 9gh0 9ghas 9ghdf 9ghgh 9gh 91 92 93

35. pages; 30 pills; 40 papers the man caught 26 pike, 15 roach,

36. 36 toddlers and 2 plaice played 3 turns in cricket match.

37. He has got 663 marks of out 700 in the final examination.

38.	Alishba is very hard-working but did get 2.94 CGPA in final.

39.	There are 3360 gallon of water in the tank.

40.	A cube of side 2cm is placed in a graduated cylinder.

41.	Write 0.00167 m and 26300 kg in standard form.

42.	The Goldsmith weighed the mass of potassium as 600 mg

43.	Diameter of HIV=0.000,0001m, 7 nanometre, 96 megawatt

44.	Diameter of the sun = 1000000000 m

45.	A brick fall from the Bab-e-khyber 15 m high.

46.	The velocity of a truck increases in 20 s from 10m per second.

47.	A runner makes one lap around a 260 m circular track in a time

48.	A bus travel 15km towards west and makes of 10km distance.

49.	A 30kg object is supported from rope find the tension.

50.	Main aspects of the economic reforms during 1971.

51.	The election of 2002 and restoration of democracy.

52.	More than 313 servants were disqualified due to corruption.

53.	Government employees were allowed to keep up to 100 acres.

54.	The bonus scheme implemented in 1959 was abolished.

55.	Senate is a permanent institution comprising of 104 members.

56.	The nuclear energy program started in 1954.

57.	Total members of each Union Council were 21.

58.	Polling stations were setup for 72 million registered voters.

59.	India demonstrated nuclear explosions in 1974 and 1998.

60.	About 50 thousand refugees were forced to migrate.

61.	In case B a force of 100 N makes an angle of 45 degree.

62. A force of 100 N is applied perpendicularly at a distance of 0.50

63. The weight of the materials is 10,000 N and 150000N.

64. A satellite is revolving around the Earth at a height of 44000km

65. Mass of woman is 100 kg and mass of child 25 kg.

66. Lifting a 50kg barbell straight up 1.95 m.

67. Calculate the gravitational potential energy of a 2000 kg piano.

68. An elevator weighing 5000N is raised to a height of 15.0m

69. A ski-hill chair lift that transports 500 people per hour.

70. It takes a 27504M motor to lift a 385kg sofa set.

71. Team A pulls B by applying a force of 1100N to the rope.

72. A bullet of mass 30g travels at a speed of 400m per second.

73. A mass of 10 kg is lifted vertically through a height of 5m.

74. The electric heater is heated at 250W.

75. If a petrol engine does 20 J of useful work for every 100J.

76. Hira weighing 500 N takes 90 s to reach the top of a hill 18m.

77. A machine lifts 200 kg of bricks vertically up to height of 30 m.

78. A weight of 30 N is hung from a wire of original length 2.0 m

79. A diamond has a volume of 0,00002 m3

80. A block of concrete is 900 11 and its base is a square of 3m,

81. the pressure at a depth of 100m below the surface of water

82. An elastic wire of length 2m and cross sectional area

83. A railway line 1200 km long is laid at 25 degree centigrade.

84. A brass disc at 293 K has a diameter of 0.30m

85. 0.5 kg of copper needs 1950 J of heat.

LESSON 10

PUNCTUATION & SYMBOLS KEYS ➤

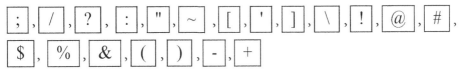

Note:

- For most of the punctuation and symbols keys you must hold down the **Shift** key and then press the corresponding punctuation or symbol key.
- It is recommended to repeat this lesson a few times.

1. [[[[[n [[; [[b [[/ [[e [[? [[: [[~ [n[[nn [n; [nb [n / [ne [n ? [n : [n~ [;[

2. [;n [;; [;b [; / [;e [; ? [; : [;~ [b[[bn [b; [bb [b / [be [b ? [b : [b~ [/[[/n

3. [/; [/b [/ / [/e [/ ? [/ : [/~ [e[[en [e; [eb [e / [ee [e ? [e : [e~ [?[[

4. ?n [?; [?b [? / [?e [?? [?: [?~ [:[[:n [:; [:b [: / [:e [: ? [: : [:

5. ~ [~ [[~ n [~; [~ b [~ / [~ e [~ ? [~ : [~ ~ n[[n[n n[; n[b n[/ n[e

6. n[? n[: n[~ nn[nnn nn; nnb nn / nne nn ? nn : nn~ n;[n;n n;; n;b n;

7. / n;e n; ? n; : n;~ nb[nbn nb; nbb nb / nbe nb ? nb : nb~ n /[n /n n

8. /; n /b n / / n /e n / ? n / : n /~ ne[nen ne; neb ne / nee ne ? ne : 7:30pm

9. ne~ n ?[n ?n n ?; n ?b n ? / n ?e n ?? n ?: n ?~ n : [following words:

10. !!! !!! !!! !!! aaa aaa aaa aaa !!! aaa !!! aaa !!! aaa !a! !a! aaa !a! !a! aaa !a! !a! aaa

11. --- --- --- --- ;;; ;;; ;;; ;;; --- ;;; --- ;;; --- ;;; -;- -;- -;- -;- ;-; ;-; -;- ;-; ;-; -;- ;-; ;-; -;

12. That's green, away from all mankind; Otherwise; hold everything tight.

13. """" '" '" '" '" '" '" '" '"" '" '" '" '" '" '" '"" '" "No," said Motti; I will be true to my master."

14. ;;, ./. ./. /./ /./ ; , . / ; , . / ;,./ ;,./ ;/,. ;/,. ;;; ,,, ... /// ;;; ;-; ;/; ;;; ;-; ; / ; ; , ; ; / ; ; , ;

15. /?/ /?/ ??? ??? ??? /// /// /// ?/ ?/ ?/ /? /? /? ?? // ?/ /? /? /? /? /? /? /? /? /? /? /?

16. @ @ ? @ @ ? @ @ ? # # @ # # ? # # @ # # ? # # ; # # ; # @ @ # @ @ # @ @ # # #

17. # # #! # # !# # # ! # # # @ @ / @ @ / @ @ / @ @ ~ # @# @# @# @# @# @ / / /

18. ?e ??? ??: ??~ ?:[?:n ?:; ?:b ?: / ?:e ?: ? ?: : ?:~ ?:~ ?:

19. ?~ [?~ n ?~; ?~ b ?~ / ?~ e ?~ ? ?~ : ?~ ~ :[[:[n :[; :[b :[b :[b :

20. [/ : [e : [? : [: : [~ :n[:nn :n; :nb :n / :ne :n ? :n: :n~ : :n~

21. en :e; :eb :e / :ee :e ? :e: :e~ :\t \n \t \n @? @? # ~ ? ! ? eng: com:

22. & & & & & & & & = = = = = = = = = = = = ( ) ( ) ( ) ( ) ( ) ( ) ( ) ( ) ( ) ( ) ( )

23. & & & & & & & & & & & & & $$$ $$$ $ $ $ $ $ $$ $$ $$ $$$ & = & = & =

24. @(#)&@ @(#)&@ @(#)&@ @(#)&@ @(#)&@ @(#)&@ && @ & @ & @ &

25. (=) (=) (=) (=) (=) (0) (=) (1) (=) (2) (=) (3) (=) (4) (=) (5) (=) (6) (=) (7)

26. a!a a!a !!! !!! !!! aaa aaa aaa !a !a !a a! a! a! !! aa !a Hurrah! alas! Ah! No! Oh!

27. Look! Oh! It's too high. Give over making that noise! Your perfume stinks!

28. ;;; ;;; ;;; -; -; -; ;- ;- ;- -- ;; -; ;- ;- -; -- -; ;; ;- - - - - ; ; ; ; - ; ; - ; ; ; ; - ; ; - ; ; ; ; - ;

29. ? ? / / / / ? / / ? ? / / ? ? /? ??/ /?? //? ?// /// ??? /?/ /// ??? /?/ /? #? #/ ! #~ ! @ # $

30. ;;- -;; ;;; --- ;-; ;;- -;; ;;; --- ;-; ;;- -;; ;;; --- ;-; ;;- -;; ;;; --- ;-; ;;- -;; ;;; --- ;-; -;; ;;; --- ;-

31. ~\ ~\ ~\ ~/// ~/// ~//~~//[~] ~/// ~\\\ ~/// ~\\\ ~/// //\\ #/ @ /~ #/ @/~

32. "" ""+ "" "+' "++ "+ "" "+ " "+" '+'+ '+' '++' '+++ '++ '+' '++ '+ " "+ " "+" "+ "+ "

33. '+' '++ '+ " "+ ' +" +"+ +" +"+ '+'+ '+'++ +'+ +" '+'+ +' ++" ++'+ ++' +++' ++++'"

34. +++' ++++ +++ ++' +++ ++ +" '+'+ +' ++' +++ ++ +' ++ + '" (3) (=) @ ? @

35. enb en / ene en ? en : en~ e;[e;n e;; e;b e; / e;e e; ? e; : e;~ eb[ebn @ ? @

36. eb; ebb eb / ebe eb ? eb : eb~ e /[e /n e /; e /b e / / e /e e / ? e / : e

37. /~ ee[een ee; eeb ee / eee ee ? ee : ee~ e ?[e ?n e ?; e ?b e ? / e ?e e ?

38. C:\Users\Public\Documents\Corel\Content X7\Fills\Typing

39. ~30 minutes before, "x ~ y" , ~42 , 12~15 , https://, https://www

40. author@example.com arrayz[@66] user@host @umar @gmail.com

41. He said, "I have got a toothache". He said, "I have got a toothache".

42. My best friend and his family, are moving to Swat. Is He not going?

43. "No, no, no, no!" exclaimed John. "No, no, no, no!" exclaimed John.

44. The cake was finished; Shireen had spent hours baking it.

45. New keys learned: ':', '?', '"', '""', '!', '-'. Isn't that awesome! Let! Excellent?

46. Congratulations -- did you think it'd be so easy? He returned home--where

47. Yes? or No? or Maybe? I'll wager it was "a bit difficult than other keys."

48. Unluckily, a lot of people don't learn to "correctly" type these keys;

49. that's a disgrace because – although though they aren't letters – Bingo!

50. they're used so often! I think you are agreed? He cried at once Wolf! Wolf!

51. "Be who you are and say what you feel because those who mind don't matter and those who matter don't mind" , "The grapes are sour."

52. "Two things are infinite: the universe and human stupidity; however;

53. Adora & Co. Barristers had a new building built at a price of $619,000.

54. This building is situated at 100 Street, New York, US.

55. You can find more info: about this firm on their website: https://typing12.com and send an email to them at info@typing12.com , contact author at typing12lessons@gmail.com

56. These are my favorite colors: purple, turquoise, and pink.

57. I bought a lot of grocery at the store: bread, meat, and chicken.

58. The writing class covers: grammar, punctuation, style, and voice.

59. The teacher asked us to bring the following: paper, oil paints, and canvas.

60. My brother's favorite fruits are the following: mango, orange, and grapes.

61. I can't believe Jane said, "I'm not coming." "The down a Walk"

62. His standard answer was "I don't know." It is called an "impossible man"

63. The man said it best: "We are not afraid." "You are free to go to your home"

64. Set X=1, FACTORIAL=1, X=X+1 [PRINT R1 and go to Step 8.]

65. If X=0 and Y=0 then PRINT "No root exists" Set MUL = NUM % A

66. If MARKS >=80 then set GRADE = "A+" else GRADE = "A"

67. If NUM%1=0 then Write "Not a Prim Number" and goto Step 7

68. Python, C++, Objective-C, Java, Swift, C# and Ruby   are significant

69. #define AGE 10, float accountBalance=5353.87; char grade = 'A'

70. Floating type variables can hold real numbers such as: 2.34, -9.382, 5.0

71. char title[30]= "Author: Muhammad Umar", char book[40] = "Typing";

72. ALGOL, Pascal, PL/I and Ada are examples of structured languages.

73. Escape sequences are \new, \t, \n, \line, \v, \r, \b \n \n \t \v \r \b \t \r \n \n

74. gets ( ) function reads characters from the standard input (stdin).

75. +=, -=, *=, /=, \=, &= are compound assignment operators.

76. ~ (bitwise complement), (~A) = -61, i.e,. 1100 0011 in 2's form.

77. %c %d, %i %u %o %x, %X %e, %E, %f %s <head> <body> <href></p>

78. scanf("format",&var); scanf("%s %d", str, &i); scanf("%s", str1);

79. Initial velocity, vi = 15 m/s, Final velocity, vf = 7 m/s and a=?

80. Distance covered, S = 90m, Acceleration = a = ? a car at speed of 60km/h

LESSON 11

PARAGRAPHS

Note:

- In this lesson, all the alphabets and some punctuation keys are used.
- Press **Enter** key twice to leave an additional blank line after each paragraph.
- For first line indentation, press **Tab** key with the left little finger. Note that the **Tab** key is used to insert **five** spaces at once.
- Use **Backspace** or **Delete** key to correct a mistyped word.

Once there lived a poor gardener in a certain village. One day, he was spading in his garden, all of a sudden, he found a box full of treasure. He was much delighted and brought the treasure home. Someone informed the chief minister and he claimed the treasure for himself. The poor gardener could not do anything. The chief minister took the treasure and announced himself the owner, the gardener went and informed the caliph. The caliph intervened and ordered the chief minister to hand over the treasure to the gardener.

Well, we agreed that night that we would meet here again exactly after twenty years from that date and time, no matter what our conditions might be or from what distance we might have to come. We figured out that in twenty years each of us ought to have our destiny worked out and our fortunes made, whatever they were going to be."

The few foot passengers astir in this quarter hurried dismally and silently along with coat collars turned high and pocketed hands. And in the door of the hardware store the man who had come a thousand miles to fill an appointment, uncertain almost to absurdity, with the friend of his youth, smoked his cigar and waited.

Yesterday was the opening of the Space Building here at the World's Fair. Many famous scientists, architects, and diplomats were present. There was something for everybody.

Messrs. Wood, Glass and Stone, who are the architects of the building, attended the ceremonies. The building which looks like a big glass cube is as modern as its exhibition.

A large crowd listened to the many speeches of the diplomats. Among the listeners was a little boy. He was about seven years old, had curly, black hair and big brown eyes, and was eating an ice cream sandwich. "Are you enjoying the speeches?" I asked. "No," he said, "they are boring." "Then why are you here?" "Because it's not as boring as home". There you have it. Another day at the Fair.

A preposition is a word used with a noun or a pronoun. Prepositions are words such as: of, in, on, by, from, over, besides, under, upon, into, at, around, at, with, up, down, beneath, below.

Her other many awards and medals include the Jane Adam's Medal in 1950 (USA), Woman of Achievement Medal 1950 (USA), Mother of Pakistan in 1950 (USA), Nishan-I-Imtiaz in 1959, Grand Cross of Orange Nassau in 1961 (the Netherlands), International Gimbel Award 1961-62 , Woman of the World in 1965 chosen by the Turkish Women's Association, Ankara and Cavaliere di Gran Croce in 1966 (Italy).

Purposefully, then, she walked out of the garden. Across the road and towards the children's playground in the park. The swings, roundabouts and slippery slides were set in sand to soften the children's falls. Large trees gave shade and many flowerbeds were bright around the perimeter here and there. Dumps of scarlet flowers attracted the birds, who danced and chattered in their branches.

MORE PARAGRAPHS

Note:

- In this lesson, all the alphabets and some punctuation keys are used.
- Press **Enter** key twice to leave an additional blank line after each paragraph.
- For first line indentation, press **Tab** key with the left little finger. Note that the **Tab** key is used to insert **five** spaces at once.
- Use **Backspace** or **Delete** key to correct a mistyped word.

Waiting for the class the other day, I was touched to witness a boy who was visually impaired being escorted into a class by his class fellow and led to the sink so that he could wash his hands. His friend patiently guided the boy through the process with care and concern and then led him slowly back to the classroom. It was a totally unexpected moment of joy for me. This child just lit up with a huge smile and an energy that I will never forget.

The world of living things can be grouped according to similarities and differences. Animal scientists do this by studying how members of the animal kingdom are alike. This is not always an easy task. Even within the same group of animals, there may be surprising differences. For example, while most mammals are land-living animals, some like the bats are flying creatures. The aquatic mammals, such as the whale and the dolphin, move from place to place by swimming. Others, like the mole, are digging animals that use their burrows for escaping from predators. Therefore, the animals' 'moving in different ways' is not a very useful method of classifying them. Instead, scientists rely on the classifying of a wider group of features, such as whether the animal has a backbone (vertebrates) or not (invertebrates).

Nasiruddin is a character who appears in many stories, always witty, sometimes wise, even philosophic, sometimes the instigator of practical jokes on others and often a fool or the butt of a joke. Stories relating to Nasiruddin are generally humorous, but in the subtle humor, there is always a lesson to be learned. These stories involve people and incidents in all walks of life, including kings, beggars, politicians, clerics etc. He is known by different names in different countries.

Our residential area has a number of issues including the problem of cleanliness. A few days ago, I contacted a few residents of the area including elders and the youth, organized them into a group and launched a cleanliness campaign in the area.

Generosity means goodness and kind-heartedness. Generosity means spending money, time and energies with an open hand and heart. It is freely sharing what you have with others. It is being willing to offer money, help or time when it is needed. To be generous means giving something that is valuable to you without expectation of reward or return. Many traditions measure generosity not by the size of the gift, but by what it cost the giver. It is natural that everyone wants to keep the valuable things for himself, but Allah Al-Mighty has ordered us to spend the things dearer to us.

Zarin Gul was a strong man of sixty-five. He was serious and hard working. He was an expert in his work. He starved himself to death due to self-respect. His shop was in a busy street in Qissa Khwani Bazar. A big sized Peshawari chappal overhung on the wooden door of his shop. The inside of his shop was quiet and serene like a sacred place. A big smooth square-shaped stone, a heavy wooden mallet, an awl, and three-legged anvil were inside the shop.

Modern electronic equipment have been discovered which have improved the quality of treatment people receive at the health institutions as well as increasing their survival chances from various ailments. Another notable benefit of technology is that it has enabled doctors to discover most health problems while they are still in the developing stages and treat them before they develop into advance stages.

Stepping into the 21st century, almost everybody is living on the edge of technological and scientific advancements. Many inventions and discoveries have been made by so many great minds whose purposes were to make our life always better than before.

A 'natural disaster' is a major event resulting from natural processes. It causes a great loss of life and property. During such disasters, the number of affected people, tripled and houseless is more than the number of people who lose their lives. Even the economy of the place gets affected.

LESSON 12

SHORT STORIES

Note:

- In this lesson, all the alphabets and some punctuation keys are used.
- Press **Enter** key twice to leave an additional blank line after each paragraph.
- Type the title of the story in **capital** and **align** as center by either using **Center** align option or press **Ctrl+E** if you are on word processor.
- For first line indentation, press **Tab** key with left little finger.
- Use **Backspace** or **Delete** key to correct a mistyped word.

THE STRANGE VOYAGE

I had inherited considerable wealth from my parents but being young and foolish, I wasted it carelessly. Finding that riches speedily take to themselves wings if managed badly, I began to think of how I could make the best of what still remained to me. I sold all my household goods by public auction and joined a company of merchants who traded by sea. I obtained goods as were suitable it for the places I intended to visit and embarked in a good ship with other merchants. We went from island to island, often making excellent bargains, until one day we landed at a spot which, though covered with fruit trees and springs of excellent water, appeared to possess neither houses nor people. While my companions wandered here and there gathering flowers and fruit I sat down in a shady place, and, having heartily enjoyed the provisions I had brought with me, I fell asleep.

How long I slept I do not know but when I opened my eyes and started to my feet I perceived with horror that I was alone and that the ship was gone. I ran here and there in despair, and found that the ship I sailed in has left the shore. I took courage and looked for means of escape. I climbed a tall tree and looked towards the sea but finding nothing hopeful there, I turned landward and curiosity was excited by a huge dazzling white object, so far off that I could not make out what it might be.

Descending from the tree, I hastily collected what remained of my provisions and set off as fast as I could go towards it. As I drew near it seemed to me to be a white ball of immense size and height and when I touched it, I found it marvelously smooth and soft.

As it was impossible to climb it —for it presented no foot-hold — I walked around about it seeking some opening, but there was none. By this time the sun was near setting, but quite suddenly it fell dark, something like a huge black cloud came swiftly over me, and I saw with amazement that it was a bird of extraordinary size which was hovering near. Then I remembered that I had often heard the sailors speak of a wonderful bird called a Roc, and it occurred to me that the white object which had so puzzled me must be its egg.

Sure enough, the bird settled slowly down upon it, covering it with its wings to keep it warm, and I sat close beside the egg in such a position that one of the bird's feet, which was as large as the trunk of a tree, was just in front of me.

Taking off my turban I tied myself securely to it with the hope that the Roc, when it took flight next morning, would bear me away with it from the deserted island.

As soon as the down appeared the bird rose into the air carrying me up and up till I could no longer see the earth, and then suddenly it descended so quickly that I lost consciousness. When I became aware that the Roc had settled and that I was once again upon solid ground, I hastily untied my turban from its foot and freed myself.

The valley in which I found myself was deep and narrow, and surrounded by mountains which towered into the clouds and were so steep and rocky that there was no way of climbing up their sides. As I wandered about, seeking anxiously for some means of escaping from this trap, I observed that the ground was covered with diamonds. This sight gave me great pleasure, but my delight was speedily damped when I saw also numbers of horrible snakes so long and so large that the smallest of them could have swallowed an elephant with ease. Fortunately for me, they seemed to hide in caves of the rocks by day and only came out by night, probably because of their enemy the Roc.

All day long I wandered up and down the valley, and when it grew dusk I crept into a little cave and, having blocked up the entrance to it with a stone, I ate part of my little store of food and lay down to sleep, but all through the night the serpents crawled to and from, hissing horribly. In the morning when the snakes went to their dens, I came tremblingly out of my cave and wandered up and down the valley once more, kicking the diamonds contemptuously out of my path, for I felt that they were indeed vain things to a man in my situation.

At last, I sat down upon a rock, but I had hardly closed my eyes when I was startled by something which fell to the ground with a thud close beside me. It was a huge piece of fresh meat, and as I stared at it several more pieces rolled over the cliffs in different places. It was the merchants throwing great lumps of meat into the valley which fell with so much force upon the diamonds that they stuck to it. When the eagles pounced upon the meat and carried it off to their nests to feed their hungry children, the merchants would scare the eagle away and secure the treasure.

I had an idea and I began by picking up all the largest diamonds I could find and storing them carefully in the bag which had held my provisions; this I tied securely to my belt I then chose the piece of meat which seemed most suited to my purpose and, with the aid of my turban, bound it firmly to my back, this done I laid down upon my face and awaited the coming of the eagles. I soon heard the flapping of their mighty wings above me and had the satisfaction of feeling one of them seize upon my piece of meat, and me with it, and rise slowly towards his nest, into which he presently dropped me.

Luckily for me the merchants were on the watch and setting up their usual outcries, they rushed to the nest scaring away the eagle. Their amazement was great when they discovered me. I made a deal with them by showing them the diamonds I had brought from the valley. The merchants agreed to take me along, I stayed with them for several days, and then as they were journeying homewards, I gladly accompanied them. Before we left I exchanged one of my diamonds for much goodly merchandise by which I profited greatly on our homeward way. At last I reached home, where my first action was to bestow large sums of money upon the poor, after which I settled down to enjoy tranquility the riches I had gained with so much toil and pain.

THE HOUSE A CARPENTER BUILT FOR HIMSELF

Antonio was a carpenter who built houses in towns and villages. He built most of the houses for the people who lived in his village. He was a gifted carpenter Unfortunately, he was never able to afford a home of his own. Now it was time for the elderly carpenter to retire from the company he was working for on his last working day his boss asked him, " Antonio, what are your plans after

The carpenter said, "Sir, after leaving house building business, I want to build a house for myself and live a more leisurely life with my family.

 Antonio added further. I would miss the paycheck, but after all, it's time to retire."

The boss was sorry to see his good worker go and asked, "Antonio could you build just one more house as a personal favor?"

The boss further added I want you to build the finest house you are capable of, and I want you to spare no expense, for I intend to give this home to a dear friend.

Antonio agreed to the job and was about to begin when a thought struck him:

This wealthy man already has a few houses. I do not have my own. I will use the inferior material, cut a few corners and do a quick job on the house, make it looks really nice, and charge him the full amount. That way I can pocket the leftover money and finally afford to build my own house." He resorted to shoddy workmanship and used inferior materials. It was an unfortunate way to end his career. When the carpenter finished his work, the boss went to view the house and was impressed it looked beautiful from a distance. The boss turned to the crooked carpenter and said, "The house looks wonderful, I am so glad that you spared no expense, as I told you earlier I intend to give this home to a dear friend who deserves a house like this one.

"The boss shook the carpenter's hand, and with a huge smile gave him an envelope with a thank-you card and a folded piece of paper. The carpenter was disdainful - until he unfolded the paper and found the deed to the house he had just built with that, he handed the keys over to the carpenter and said, "Here is your new home, my friend, my gift to you because you have been working with me for a long time".

 This act of kindness greatly shocked the carpenter. He was ashamed of himself and was repenting on the fact that he not only betrayed his friend but also compromised on his integrity and honesty. Consequently, he had to live in a house for the rest of his life which he had built so carelessly. If he had not dishonored his uprightness and virtues he would have been living in a house of perfection and beauty. Imagine yourself as the carpenter and the house as your character. It is built by your choices and actions. Deceit, fraud, and dishonesty are like the low-quality materials that the carpenter has used in-house. The result will be creaky floor, leaky roof and fragile foundation carelessly, and with inferior material, deceit and in reactions rather than action.

At a critical moment of our lives, we put up less than the best and then look with shock at the situation which we have created with our follies and blunders. As result, we are living in a house which we have built with our own actions and reactions.

If we had done honestly, we would have not been feeling sorry for our folly and foibles. Similarly, if we're not happy with what we see in our country, perhaps it's a direct consequence of what we've been building over the years. Thus, ask not what our country can do for us, ask what we can do for our country.

THE FARMER'S DOG

A farmer had a faithful dog, Motti, who had grown very old and had lost all his teeth. And one day, when the farmer and his wife were standing together before the house the farmer said, "I will abandon old Motti at the train station tomorrow morning, for he is of no use now." But his wife said, "No! Let the poor faithful creature live with us; he has served us well a great many years, and we ought to give him a livelihood for the rest of his days."

"But what can we do with him?" said the farmer, "he has not a tooth in his mouth, and the thieves don't care for him at all, to be sure he has served us, but then he did it to earn his livelihood; tomorrow shall be his last day, depend upon it."

Poor Motti, who was lying close by them, heard all that the farmer and his wife said to one another, and was very much frightened to think tomorrow would be his last day, so in the evening he went to his good friend the wolf, who lived in the woods, and told him all his sorrows, and how his master meant to kill him in the morning. "

Make yourself easy," said the wolf, "I will give you some good advice. Your master, you know, goes out every morning very early with his wife into the field; and they take their little child with them, and lay it down behind the hedge in the shade while they are at work. You lie down close by the child and pretend to be watching it, and I will come out of the wood and run away with it; you must run after me as fast as you can, and I will let it drop, then you may carry it back, and they will think you have saved their child, and will be so thankful to you that they will take care of you as long as you live."

The dog liked this plan very well, and accordingly so it was managed. The wolf ran with the child a little way; the farmer and his wife screamed out, but Motti soon overtook him and carried the poor little thing back to his master and mistress.

Then the farmer patted him on the head, and said, "Old Motti has saved our child from the wolf, and therefore he shall live and be well taken care of, and have plenty to eat. Wife, go home, and give him a good dinner, and let him have my old cushion to sleep on as long as he lives." So from this time forward, Motti had all that he could wish for.

 Soon afterward the wolf came and wished him joy, and said, "Now, my good fellow, you must tell no tales, but turn your head the other way when I want to taste one of the old farmer's fine fat sheep."

"No," said Motti; I will be true to my master."

However, the wolf thought he was in joke, and came one night to get a dainty morsel. But Motti had told his master what the wolf meant to do; so he laid wait for him behind the barn door, and when the wolf was busy looking out for a good fat sheep, he had a stout cudgel laid about his back, that combed his locks for him finely.

 Then the wolf was very angry, and called Motti "an old rogue," and swore he would have his revenge. So the next morning the wolf sent the bear to challenge Motti to come into the wood to fight the matter. Now Motti had nobody he could ask to be his second but the farmer's old three-legged cat, so he took her with him, and as the poor thing limped along with some trouble, she stuck up her tail straight in the air.

The wolf and the wild bear were first on the ground; and when they espied their enemies coming, and saw the cat's long tail standing straight in the air, they thought she was carrying a sword for Motti to fight with; and every time she limped, they thought she was picking up a stone to throw at them; so they said they should not like this way of fighting, and the bear lay down behind a bush, and the wolf jumped up into a tree. Motti and the cat soon came up and looked about and wondered that no one was there. The bear, however, had not quite hidden himself, for his ears stuck out of the bush, and when he shook one of them a little, the cat, seeing something move, and thinking it was a mouse, sprang upon it, and bit and scratched it, so that the bear jumped up and ran away, shouting out, "Look up in the tree, there sits the one who is to blame." So, they looked up and espied the wolf sitting amongst the branches, and they called him a coward and would not suffer him to come down till he was heartily ashamed of himself and had promised to be good friends again with old Motti.

CHAPTER 6

IMPORTANT SYMBOLS AND GENERAL RULES

Capitalization

Capitalization means to type the first letter in uppercase. For a single capital letter use any one of the shift keys but when an entire sentence or a group of words are in capital then the best way is to use the Caps Lock key. Pressing the Caps Lock will show a light, indicating that Caps Lock is turned on. To turn it off, press again. As we have discussed earlier, the basic rule is; if the letter to be typed is from the right hand then use the shift key with the left hand and vice versa.

Consider the following **rules** for the use of capital letters:

- A sentence always starts with a capital letter.
- The letter 'I' when referring to the subject pronoun should always be capitalized when talking about yourself.
- Direct speech should start with a capital letter.
- The name of a person, place and proper noun should be capitalized.
- Names of books, films etc. are typed in capital letters.
- Always type names of days and months in capital letters.
- Names of seasons should NOT be capitalized.

Look at the following examples:

1. **Although** he invited me, **I** did not come.
2. **He** ordered his son, "Bring a glass of water."
3. The name of the company was **HAMAYUN ENGINEERING FIRM**.
4. Add **THREE** potatoes and **TWO** teaspoons of salt to the mixture.
5. **I** will meet my best friend on Sunday.
6. **I** am going to **Saudi** Arabia in July.
7. The latest book by **Muhammad Umar** is called **'Learn Touch Typing in 12 Simple Lessons'**.

Hyphens and dashes

The hyphen is a punctuation sign that finds its place between two words, e.g. rock-forming, or it is used in place of the word 'to', e.g. 15-17 High School Street. It does not require space on either side. The dash is used for a break or a pause. It is frequently used as a substitute for brackets or a comma. Unlike hyphen, it requires space on both sides.

Look at the following examples:

1. The **re-canceling** of the meeting was felt badly.
2. This textbook has **twenty-two** chapters.
3. You can expect your product from **1-8** January.
4. After dinner, we visited my **great-grandmother**.
5. Ali's dad is **thirty-seven years old**.
6. Jacky is my **well-trained** dog.
7. **One-third** of the people did not show up for the event.
8. The **Beach-boys** ---a popular 60's band --- gave a performance.

Exclamation mark

The exclamation mark is used to express humor, emphasis, sorrow or joy in a sentence or paragraph.

Look at the following:

1. **Hurrah!** We have won the match.
2. **Oops!** Something went wrong.
3. **Hurry up!** The sale is ending.
4. What a silly girl you are! Fancy falling over in the playground.
5. **Bravo!** You have really done so very well.
6. Alice said, "how clever I am!'

Question mark

A question mark is placed at the end of a sentence which asks a question. Sometimes, it is also used in business letters to show a query on a date, event or time etc.

Look at the following:

1. Where are you going now?

2. Does this mean he will never come again?

3. Are you thinking of quitting your current job?

4. Do you know the reason why our offer was rejected?

5. Are you able to drive a tractor?

6. Have you applied for this position?

Square brackets

[ ] are called square brackets and they are hardly used. The practical use of square brackets is to show addition to a direct quotation:

Look at the following example:

1. Mr. Yasir said in his report: 'I am so sorry about the lack of pay rise this year, but I hope that you [the employees] will understand the situation.'

Quotation marks

The single or double quotation marks are used for quotations or direct speech.

Look at the following example:

1. "My research paper for final year is 'Cloud DBMS'," said Hilal.

2. The animals' "moving in different ways" is not a very useful method of classifying them.

3. When we intentionally "live below our means" and avoid overcommitment.

Apostrophes

' is known as Apostrophes and used to show possession or omission. Apostrophes are also used for shortening certain words. Keep in mind, it is the same symbol as the single quotation mark.

1. The car's owner has been fined $200 for using a mobile while driving.
2. I won't buy a new laptop.
3. Your shoes are the prettiest I've seen. They're so cool.
4. The dog hurt its paw. It's a good thing that you were there.
5. The children's homework is hard. They've got lots to do.

Oblique, solidus or slash

Oblique or simply slash is used for references or to show options.

Look at the following example:

1. I have typed a personal narrative/autobiography.
2. Identify a real-life situation/problem that could be improved with generosity.
3. It has 31 births /1000 according to 2009 censuses.

Ampersand

The '&' symbol is called ampersand and should only be used in company names, in accepted abbreviations, or in tables where there is no space.

Look at the following examples:

1. Adora & Brothers, together with Angela & Son, came today.
2. E & OE, if on forms means Errors and Omissions Excepted.
3. At the far end of the wall of the shop was hanging a small signboard, showing Zarin Gul & Brothers.
4. Practical steps are needed to preserve the flora & fauna of the country.

CHAPTER 7

TYPING QUIZZES

TOUCH TYPING QUIZZES FOR SELF ASSESSMENTS

Let's take some quick typing quizzes to know about how much knowledge we have gained about touch typing. Note that these typing quizzes are based on the QWERTY layout of the keyboard.

There are five quizzes.

- Quiz 1 covers "Home Row" keys.
- Quiz 2 contains questions on Top row keys.
- Quiz 3 and Quiz 4 comprise 10 questions which cover "Bottom Row" keys and alphanumeric keys respectively.
- Quiz 5 has 20 questions which cover all keys including alphabet, alphanumeric and numbers keys.

In total, there are 70 questions. Each question has four possible answers (options). Choose the correct answer and then compare it against answers given on page 129.

You can also submit these quizzes online where your answers are automatically checked and graded accordingly. Follow this link to take the quizzes online.

__Typing12.com/typing-quizzes__

QUIZ – 1

Note:

- This Quiz is based on the **QWERTY** keyboard layout.
- It covers Home Row keys ➤ **A,S,D,F,G,H,J,K,L**
- There are **15** Multiple Choice Questions.
- Answers on page **101**.

1. Which of the following fingers can be used to type letter **D**?

   A. Middle finger
   B. Little finger (Pinky)

   C. Thumb
   D. Lady finger

2. Which key is assigned to the **ring finger** of the right hand?

   A. D
   B. L

   C. S
   D. I

3. In touch typing the word "**Added**" can be typed using only _____ hand fingers.

   A. Right
   B. Left

   C. Both
   D. Either right or left

4. Which finger is assigned to letter **S**?

   A. Lady finger
   B. Middle finger

   C. Ring finger
   D. Little finger

5. The letter "**K**" is associated with which one of the following fingers?

   A. Little finger
   B. Ring finger

   C. Middle finger
   D. Lady finger

6. The letters **A, S** and **F** are associated with _____ hand?

   A. Right
   B. Left

   C. Both
   D. None

7. The **Home Keys** for right hand are:

   A. ASDF
   B. J, K, L, ;

   C. Q,W,E,R
   D. U,I,O,P

91

8. Which of the following keys usually have **bumps**?

    A. A,S

    B. K,l

    C. F,J

    D. GH

9. To type **space**, we can use _____ **thumb**.

    A. Right

    B. Left

    C. Both

    D. Right or left

10. The **Home Keys** for left hand are:

    A. A,S,D,F

    B. J, K,L,;

    C. U,I,O,P

    D. Q,W,E,R

11. Which of the following keys belongs to **Home** row?

    A. A,S,D,F,J,K,L

    B. F,D,S,A,L,K,J

    C. A,S,D,F,G,H,J,K,L;

    D. A,S,D,F,G,H,K,L

12. The words **"add"** and **"dad"** can be typed by only _____ hand?

    A. Right

    B. Left

    C. Both

    D. Either right or left

13. The letter **"G"** is assigned to the lady finger of _____ hand.

    A. Left

    B. Right

    C. Both

    D. None

14. The letter **"H"** is assigned to the lady finger of _____ hand.

    A. Both

    B. Left

    C. Right

    D. None of these

15. How many letters are there on the Home row of the QWERTY keyboard?

    A. 15

    B. 12

    C. 9

    D. 8

QUIZ – 2

Note:

- This Quiz is based on the **QWERTY** keyboard layout.
- It covers **Top** Row keys ➤ **Q,W,E,R,T,Y,U,I,O,P**
- There are **15** Multiple Choice Questions.
- Answers on page **102**.

1. Which of the following are known as "**Top row**" letters?

   A. A,S,D,F,G,H,I,J,K,L   B. Z,X,C,V,B,N,M

   C. Q,W,E,R,T,Y,U,I,O,P   D. None of these

2. The letter "**Q**" can be typed using _____ finger of the left hand.

   A. Little   B. Ring

   C. Lady   D. Middle

3. How many letters are there in the top row of the QWERTY keyboard layout?

   A. 9   B. 10

   C. 12   D. 15

4. The word "**were**" can be typed by using _____ hand(s).

   A. Both   B. Any

   C. Left   D. Right

5. Which of following rows of QWERTY keyboard has the most vowel letters i.e. **E,I,O,U**?

   A. Home row   B. Bottom row

   C. Top row   D. Both rows

6. Identify the row(s) that can be used to type the word "**Deep**"

   A. Top and bottom   B. Home and bottom

   C. Top and home   D. None of these

7. Name the finger for typing the letter "**O**" with the QWERTY layout.

   A. Lady finger   B. Middle finger

   C. Little   D. Ring finger

8. According to touch typing which letter can be typed with the **middle finger** from the top row.

    A. U   B. O

    C. L   D. I

9. Which of the following fingers is associated with the letter "**U**"?

    A. Little   B. Ring

    C. Middle   D. Lady

10. Name the only two fingers that can type the word "**POP**".

    A. Little and middle   B. Little and ring fingers

    C. Ring and lady finger   D. None of these

11. Which finger from the left hand is responsible for typing the letter "**T**"?

    A. Little finger   B. Middle finger

    C. Ring Finger   D. Lady Finger

12. Determine the correct order of fingers to typed the word "**queue**"

    A. Little >> Lady>>Middle >>Lady>>Middle

    B. Little >> Middle >>Middle >> Lady >>Little

    C. Little >> middle >> Ring >>Little>>Little

    D. Little>>Ring >>Little>> middle>> Lady

13. Which of the following fingers is reserved for letter **W**?

    A. Little   B. Ring

    C. Middle   D. Lady

Which of the following fingers will you press to type the letter "**Y**"?

    A. Either right- or left-hands' lady finger

    B. Left hand lady finger

    C. Right hand lady finger

    D. None of these

14. To type the letter "**i**" we use_____ finger.

    A. Lady   B. Ring

    C. Little   D. Middle

QUIZ – 3

Note:

- This Quiz is based on the **QWERTY** keyboard layout.
- It covers Bottom Row keys ➤ **Z,X,C,V,B,N,M,./**
- There are **10** Multiple Choice Questions.
- Answers on page **103**.

1. Which of the following keys on the QWERTY keyboard are regarded as "**Bottom row**"?

    A. A,S,D,F,G,H,J,K,L,;   B. Q,W,E,R,T,Y,U,I,O,P

    C. A,S,D,F,J,K,L;   D. Z,X,C,V,B,N,M< >?

2. Which of the following fingers is used to type the letter "**Z**"?

    A. Little (pinky)   B. Middle

    C. Thumb   D. Ring

3. Which of the following letters is assigned to the **ring finger** of the left hand from the bottom row?

    A. Z   B. D

    C. C   D. X

4. To type "**N**" we use the lady finger of _____ hand.

    A. Left   B. Right

    C. Either left or right   D. None of these

5. Which of the following fingers is responsible for typing letter "**B**"?

    A. Lady   B. Middle

    C. Ring   D. Little

6. Choose the correct order of fingers to type "**VBN**".

    A. Right lady finger ≫ left lady finger
    B. Right Lady finger ≫ Right Lady finger ≫ Left Lady finger
    C. Lady finger of either hand
    D. Left Lady finger ≫ Left Lady finger ≫ Right Lady finger

7. Right-hand **little** finger is responsible for typing_____ from bottom row.

    A. M   B. <

    C. >   D. ?

8. How many keys are there on **Bottom row**?

    A. 8   B. 9

    C. 10   D. 11

9. The "**back slash**" (/) can be typed by using the _____ finger of the right hand.

    A. Little   B. Lady

    C. Middle   D. Ring

10. The **Shift** keys can be pressed with the help of _____ fingers.

    A. Lady   B. Middle

    C. Ring   D. Little

QUIZ – 4

Note:

- This Quiz is based on **QWERTY** keyboard layout.
- It covers Alphanumeric keys ➤ Alpha-numeric (0-9,~,@,#,$,%,^,*,(,),-,_,=,+)
- There are **10** Multiple Choice Questions.
- Answers on page **103**.

1. Identify the correct sequence of fingers to type the street number "**315**".

    A. Middle ≫ Little ≫ Middle

    B. Little ≫ Middle ≫Lady

    C. Middle ≫ Little ≫Lady

    D. Lady ≫ Middle ≫ Little

2. Which of the following fingers can be used to type the number "**4**"?

    A. Ladyfinger   B. Ring finger

    C. Middle   D. Little finger

3. Name the alpha-numeric keys which are associated with lady finger of the right hand.

    A. $, %   B. ^, &

    C.),- , _, +   D. ~ ,!

4. Which of the following fingers is responsible for typing number 8 and symbol * (asterisk)?

    A. Only Middle   B. Little and middle

    C. Middle and Lady   D. Little and lady

5. Determine the correct order of fingers to enter the number "**999**".

    A. Lady ≫ Lady ≫ Lady

    B. Middle ≫ Ring ≫ Middle

    C. Ring ≫ Middle ≫ Ring

    D. Ring ≫ Ring ≫ Ring

6. Name the finger which can be used to enter the **dollar ($)** sign.

    A. Little   B. Middle

    C. Lady   D. Thumb

7. What number is typed when **ring** and **little** fingers are used from left hand?

    A. 12   B. 13

    C. 21   D. 23

8. Identify the fingers from left hand which can type the number **454**

    A. Little   B. Ring

    C. Lady   D. Middle

9. What numbers can be typed with lady finger from right hand?

    A. 4,5   B. 2,3

    C. 0,9   D. 6,7

10. The little finger of _____ hand is associated with the number 0(zero)?

    A. Right   B. Left

    C. Either right or left   D. None of these

QUIZ – 5

Note:

- This Quiz is based on the **QWERTY** keyboard layout.
- It covers All keys ➤ **A-Z, 0 - 9, symbols (~,!,@,#,$,%,^,*,(,))**
- There are **20** Multiple Choice Questions.
- Answers on page **104**.

1. According to touch typing, the keys **A,W,C,T,G** and **V** can be pressed with _____ hand.

   A. Right   B. Left

   C. Either left or right   D. None of these

2. Identify the correct order of fingers for typing the word "**saw**".

   A. Lady finger ≫ Little finger ≫ Ring finger

   B. Ring finger ≫ Little finger ≫ Ring finger

   C. Middle finger ≫ Ring finger ≫ Little finger

   D. Middle finger >> Ring finger>> Middle

3. Name the letters associated with the **lady finger** of the right hand.

   A. J,H,M,N,U,Y   B. F,G,R,T,V,B

   C. O,L   D. W,S,X

4. As per QWERTY keyboard layout the vowel letters i,o,u can be typed with _____ hand.

   A. Left   B. Right

   C. Both A and B   D. None of these

5. While touch typing the letter **U** can be typed using _____ finger.

   A. Little   B. Middle

   C. Ring   D. Lady

6. Which of the following letters can be typed with middle finger of left hand?

   A. Z   B. D

   C. B   D. K

7. Which of the following **symbols** is used when entering email address?

    A. $ B. #

    C. @   D. %

8. Which finger from the right hand is responsible for entering the **question mark (?)**?

    A. Little   B. Ring

    C. Middle   D. Lady

9. In touch typing, what is the sole purpose of the **Shift keys**?

    A. It allows to type in small letters

    B. It allows to type in both small and capital letter

    C. It allows to type in capital letters

    D. It allows to type lower case

10. On which of the following number keys, brackets i.e. ( ) are available?

    A. 1 and 2   B. 4 and 5

    C. 8 and 9   D. 9 and 0

11. To define a **gap** between words the _____ is required.

    A. Spacebar   B. Ctrl

    C. Shift   D. Alt

12. When touch typing, pressing the key associated with the ring finger from the left hand followed by pressing the key associated with the middle finger two times from top row will type _____ word.

    A. add   B. see

    C. did   D. lol

13. Which of the following keys are regarded as **home keys** associated with both hands?

    A. Q,W,E,R,Y,I,O,P   B. Z,X,C,V,N,./

    C. A,S,D,F,J,K,L,;   D. Q,A,W,S,U,J,O,L,P

14. The letter "**M**" can be typed with the help of lady finger from _____ hand.

    A. Left   B. Right

    C. Both A and B   D. Either left or right

15. The **Ctrl** and **Shift** keys are controlled with _____ finger.

    A. Little   B. Ring

    C. Middle   D. Lady

16. The _____ finger types the number **6** and **7**.

    A. Lady   B. Middle

    C. Ring   D. Little

17. Which of the following number keys types **ampersand "&"** sign while the shift key is held down?

    A. 6   B. 7

    C. 8   D. 9

18. Ring **finger** of left-hand types the _____ letter.

    A. D   B. A

    C. S   D. L

19. While touch typing, ____ finger types "**Y**" letter from top row.

    A. Lady   B. Middle

    C. Ring   D. Little

20. Which of the following keys types the **percentage (%)** symbol with shift key being held down?

    A. 4   B. 5

    C. 6   D. 7

ANSWERS

QUIZ – 1

1. The correct answer is option **A.** To type letter "D", **Middle finger** from left-hand is used.

2. The correct answer is option **B. L** key is assigned to the ring finger of the right hand.

3. The correct answer is option **B.** All characters in word "Added" belong to **Left**-hand.

4. The correct answer is option **C. Ring finger** is responsible for typing letter "S".

5. The correct answer is option **C.** The letter "K" is associated with the **Middle finger** of right-hand.

6. The correct answer is option **B.** The letters A, S and F belong to the **Left** hand.

7. The correct answer is option **B.** J, K, L, ; are known as Home row keys.

8. The correct answer is option **C.** F, J keys have jumps on them to indicate that the two index (lady) fingers should be positioned over them and other fingers on the adjacent keys.

9. The correct answer is option **D.** Either thumb i.e. **Right or left** can be used to type space.

10. The correct answer is option **A.** The home keys for the left-hand are **A, S, D,F.**

11. The correct answer is option **C. A, S, D, F, G, H, J, K ,L ,;** are the keys for both hands.

12. The correct answer is option **B.** Only **left-hand** fingers can be used to type words "add" and "dad".

13. The correct answer is option **A.** The letter "G" is assigned to the lady finger of **Left-hand.**

14. The correct answer is option **A.** The letter "H" is available on **Right-hand.**

15. The correct answer is option **C.** There are **9** keys on home row.

QUIZ – 2

1. The correct answer is option **C**. Top row letters are: **Q, W, E, R, T, Y, U, I, O, P.**

2. The correct answer is option **A**. To type letter "Q", **Little** finger of left-hand is used.

3. The correct answer is option **B**. There are **10** letters in the top row of the QWERTY keyboard layout.

4. The correct answer is option **C**. The word "were" is typed with the **Left** hand.

5. The correct answer is option **C**. The most vowels are available on the **Top row.**

6. The correct answer is option **A**. The word "deep" has letters from both **Top and Home** row.

7. The correct answer is option **D**. The letter "Q" can be typed with the **Ring finger.**

8. The correct answer is option **D**. Middle finger of right-hand type letter 'I'.

9. The correct answer is option **D**. Letter "U" is associated with the **Lady finger** of right-hand.

10. The correct answer is option **B**. The word "Pop" can be typed with only **Little and ring fingers**.

11. The correct answer is option **D**. The letter "T" is associated with **Lady Finger.**

12. The correct answer is option **A**. The correct order is as under.
    Little ≫ Lady ≫ Middle ≫ Lady ≫ Middle

13. The correct answer is option **B**. Letter "W" is associated with **Ring** finger.

14. The correct answer is option **C**. To type letter "Y", **Right hand lady finger** is used.

15. The correct answer is option **D**. Letter "i" is associated with the Middle finger of the right hand.

QUIZ – 3

1. The correct answer is option **D** which is **Z, X, C, V, B, N, M, < , > , ?.** The bottom row is just below the home row.

2. The correct answer is option **A** i.e. **Little (pinky).** The little finger from the left hand is used to type letter Z.

3. The correct answer is option **D.** The ring finger from left the hand is assigned the letter **X.**

4. The correct answer is option **B. i.e. Right**-hand lady finger is used to type the letter N.

5. The correct answer is option **A. Lady** finger is responsible for typing the letter "**B**" from the bottom row.

6. The correct answer is option **D.**
   Left Lady finger ≫ Left Lady finger ≫ Right Lady finger

7. The correct answer is option **D.** Right hand little finger is responsible to type "**?**" (question mark).

8. The correct answer is option **C.** There are **10** keys on the bottom row.

9. The correct answer is option **A.** The **Little Finger** of right-hand types the / (slash).

10. The correct answer is option **D.** The **Shift** Keys are with **Little Fingers.**

QUIZ – 4

1. The correct answer is option **C.** To enter the number "315", the correct order of keys is Middle>>Little>>Lady.

2. The correct answer is option **A.** To type number 4, **Lady finger** is used.

3. The correct answer is option **B.** The ^ and **&** signs are associated with the lady finger of the right hand.

4. The correct answer is option **A.** The number 8 and * are available on **Middle** finger.

5. The correct answer is option **A.** To enter "999", the correct order of keys is **Lady>>Lady>>Lady**

6. The correct answer is option **C.** To type dollar ($), **Lady** finger is used.

7. The correct answer is option **C. Ring** and **Little** fingers can type **"12"** number.

8. The correct answer is option **C.** To enter 454, only **Lady** finger from left hand is used.

9. The correct answer is option **D.** The lady finger from the right hand can enter **6** and **7** digits respectively.

10. The correct answer is option **A.** Zero (0) is associated with the little finger of Right hand.

QUIZ – 5

1. The correct answer is option **B.** The keys A, W, C, T, G and V are associated with **Left** hand.

2. The correct answer is option **B.** The correct order of keys for word "saw" is **Ring finger ≫ little finger ≫ Ring finger.**

3. The correct answer is option **A.** The letters associated with the lady finger are **J, H, M, N, U,** and **Y.**

4. The correct answer is option **B.** Most vowels i.e. **i, o, u** are typed with help of **Right** hand.

5. The correct answer is option **D.** Letter "U" is associated with the **Lady** finger of right hand.

6. The correct answer is option **B.** The letter **D** can be typed with middle finger of left hand.

7. The correct answer is option **C.** Every email address must contain @ symbol.

8. The correct answer is option **A.** The **Little** finger from the right hand can type the question mark.

9. The correct answer is option **C.** The **Shift** keys on both sides allow you to type in capital letters.

10. The correct answer is option **D.** The brackets i.e. ( ) are available on **9** and **0** number keys.

11. The correct answer is option **A.** To define a gap between words, the Spacebar is used.

12. The correct answer is option **B.** Pressing the key associated with the ring finger from the left hand followed by pressing the middle key two times from top row will type the word "**see**".

13. The correct answer is option **C.** The keys **A, S, D, F, J, K, L,** and **;** are known as home row keys.

14. The correct answer is option **B.** Letter "M" is associated with the lady finger of **Right** hand.

15. The correct answer is option **A.** The Ctrl and Shift keys are control with **Little** finger.

16. The correct answer is option **A.** The Lady finger types the digit 6 and 7 from the left and right hand respectively.

17. The correct answer is option **C.** The ampersand sign (&) is available on 8 number key.

18. The correct answer is option **C.** The ring finger from the left hand types letter **S.**

19. The correct answer is option **A.** From the top row, the **Lady** finger can type letter "Y".

20. The correct answer is option **B.** The number key 5 types % sign while holding down the shift key.

CHAPTER 8

WRAP UP

QUIT HUNTING AND PECKING OF KEYBOARD

Hunting and pecking mainly refer to a typing style, where a person blindly types without memorizing the keys of the keyboard. In other words, hunting and pecking of the keyboard refer to the *act of searching* for every key and then pressing it with either the index or another finger. This is because the typist has not memorized the keyboard and so may use only one or two fingers for typing any key on the keyboard, regardless of the key's position. It is also known as *chicken pecking typing*.

Disadvantages of Hunting and Pecking

Before looking at how to quit hunting and pecking, let's talk about some of the disadvantages of hunting and pecking:

1. **Divided Attention:** Hunting and pecking mean typing by keeping your eyes on the keyboard. It always keeps a person entangled towards the keys while he/she wishes to type. It not only draws your attention and forces you to look at the keyboard but also limits the thinking ability because you always look to find characters instead of focusing on work. In this method of typing, a finger can hit any key at any time, which ultimately leads to a lack of typing speed and accuracy.

2. **Spelling or Grammar Errors:** When you are typing with two fingers, you will not notice any spelling or grammar mistakes till you have made them. Touch typing allows you to edit and fix any spelling or grammar mistakes as you go. During touch typing, you can easily use the backspace key to fix them.

Things to Do to Quit Hunting and Pecking of Keyboard

Here at Typing12.com, we have assembled simple things you need to avoid and overcome hunting and pecking of the keyboard:

1. Stop Staring Down at Your Keyboard

It can be extremely tempting to stop staring down at your keyboard. But, to quit hunting and pecking habit, you need to memorize the keys of the keyboard. Touch typing can be your biggest campaigner in quitting hunting and pecking. Always keep your eyes on the screen and try to hit the right keys.

2. Learn Touch Typing

Touch typing is supposed to be a very effective way of typing which can help you to quit hunting and pecking at the keyboard with little investment of time. There are several options where you can learn touch typing. If you are looking for a book to learn touch typing and quit hunting and pecking then this book is the best option for you. It has 12 simple lessons with all the fundamentals of typing.

3. Type Daily

Typing daily will help you to cover your weak links. Try to select a particular time of day for daily practice. Do not overburden the stuff. To quit hunting and pecking, you need to learn and practice new skills. The more you practice the faster you will manage to stop hunting and pecking habits.

4. Learn Keyboard Shortcuts

Learning keyboard shortcuts is not only very handy to make your life easier but it also helps to quit hunting and pecking habits. In addition to this, utilizing keyboard shortcuts also increases typing speed and accuracy.

5. Put Stickers on Key Labels to Hide Them

This can be extremely handy for two fingers typists. If you are one of them, you stop hunting and pecking habits by putting blank stickers on key labels. So, they could be out of sight. And ultimately it will help in quitting hunting and pecking.

6. Use a Timer (Stopwatch) To Give Yourself a Challenge

Challenging yourself can be useful in quitting the habit of hunting and pecking. For this purpose, you can use a stopwatch. It will keep you active while typing. Set a time interval for typing a specific text and try to complete the typing task within the specified time interval. You will feel more alert towards achieving your goal on time. A timer will also help in increasing the typing speed with new typing habits on board.

7. Take Typing Tests to Quit Hunting and Pecking

If you are worried about typing speed after adapting new typing habits, then there is no need to be worried. The typing tests can help you to achieve your speed and gear in typing. Typing speed test will help you determine speed and accuracy after adapting to touch typing. Visit our dedicated page at ***www.typing12.com/typing-speed-test*** where you can take a free typing test to check speed and accuracy under 1 minute. Checking your typing speed before and after you have managed to quit hunting and pecking puts on the track and helps you in the decision to what to do next.

8. Stay Strong and Do Not Give Up till Quit Hunting and Pecking of Keyboard

Patience and persistence are the only keys to quitting hunting and pecking. You will have to adapt to new typing habits. This can be a struggling time for you. But you need to hold yourself for long-lasting and better results.

SOME TIPS FOR TOUCH TYPING

Do Not Look at Your Fingers

When setting for touch typing, place your fingers on the home row. Once you have done so, do not look at your finger. Looking at your finger will drastically decrease your typing speed as well as accuracy.

Keep Fingers on The Home Row

When typing a letter from the top or bottom row, you will definitely take up or bring down your finger to the corresponding key on top or button row. But make sure to relocate your finger on its home key immediately. Leaving a finger on the wrong key will lead to typing error and reduced typing speed.

Do not Look at Screen

If you are typing from paper, it is important to not look at the screen. If addicted to looking at the screen frequently, it causes you to relocate the paragraph and sentence from where you were typing. Which in turn decreases your typing accuracy and wastes the time.

In addition to this, looking at the screen also degrades typing accuracy because when you see an error you will be curious to fix it on priority.

Avoid Too Much Typing

Too much typing is also not good for physical health and performance. If you are typing with an average speed i.e. 30 WMP (Words Per Minute) for more than 2 hours you will feel tired and itching. At the same time, your finger will start hurting. If you are doing a typing job, make sure to complete your daily typing task in different intervals of time. For example, do about an hour of typing and take a small break and then start again.

Take Regular Breaks and Eye Exercise

Take regular breaks, this will reserve your physical health and future performance. Someone has said it rightly that health is wealth. If you are healthy you can earn wealth and improve your living styles. In this regard, eye exercise is equally important. Here is a simple exercise for the eye, after every 20 minutes look at far objects for 20 seconds.

SPEED OR ACCURACY

Which one is more important, speed or accuracy?

Your answer might be speed! But I am sorry to say, you have guessed wrong. The major part of touch typing is accuracy. Accuracy means to type words correctly without making any error.

If a typist can type at a very high speed and does not care about accuracy, then such typing is of no use. In other words, a typist can type more than 150 words per minute but a sequence of random letters carrying no meaning attached to them. No one will bother with this type of speed and touch typing.

Are you still concerned about speed?

Do not worry at all. Your typing speed will accelerate as you do more practice. Typing an entire book, magazine, novel, story, or any other type of document will help to achieve speed and accuracy at same time.

TIPS AND TRICKS FOR PASSING A TYPING TEST

Do you need to pass a typing test before qualifying for a job? If your answer is yes, then the proceeding list has tips and tricks for you to perform well in a typing test.

1. Practice

Preparation is a must before you opt for a typing test. Practice all the alphabets, alphanumeric and number keys. In a typing test, you can expect a combination of letters and symbols including capitalization, punctuation and hyphenation. Besides text, a typing test may contain home address,  phone number and special characters. Special characters and symbols could be /,-, @,#,$,%, (,),~ and " ". The easiest way to practice all these keys is to type from a book, magazine or newspaper. You can also check your typing speed online by visiting our dedicated page at *www.typing12.com/typing-speed-test.*

2. Take Your Keyboard with You

The keyboards in testing centers are not good and are usually obsolete. It is possible that you will not be able to type efficiently with those keyboards. To cope with this situation, if allowed, take your own keyboard with yourself. A USB keyboard will be an easy and comfortable option. Connect it to PC before starting a typing test. Now, as you are used to this keyboard, ultimately this will increase your capacity towards excellent performance and you will nail it.

3. Keep Your Fingers Warm

In winter, bare hands and fingers are exposed to cold wind; therefore they get colder than any other parts of the body. If your hands, especially your fingers, are cold, you may not be able to type with high speed and accuracy. However, you can warm up your hands and fingers in a few minutes just before taking your typing test. Wear warm gloves and massage your fingers and their tips against each other to make them warm quickly. You may put your hands under armpits or any other warm part of the body. Another idea is to blow on hands and fingers, rubbing them against each other quickly to spread the warmth across hands.

4. Get Familiar with Keyboard

If you have not brought your own keyboard, or you are not permitted to do so then get familiar with the available keyboard provided, by checking its alphabets, alphanumeric and number keys.

Find out whether all keys are functioning properly, and no key is missing or mistyping. Also, check for the keys which stick or are hard to press. The simplest way to perform a keyboard checkup is to type the sentence "The quick brown fox jumps over the lazy dog" using Notepad or any other text editor. Typing this sentence will reveal if any alphabetical key is not working fine. Next, type numbers from 0-9 and these five symbols /(slash), – (dash), _(underscore), # (number) and @ (at). If you succeed in finding out that a keyboard is not working perfectly, ask the concerned person to replace it or you can sit at any other PC with a working keyboard.

5. Do Not Get Nervous

Do not get nervous that you will perform badly. Give yourself the incentive that you can type well in front of anyone. Do not panic, relax, start typing and gradually increase your typing speed.

6. Do Not Skip Words

Many of us deem it a wise act to skip longer words during a typing test. Skipping words while typing is a very bad and ineffective idea. Ironically, it does not only decrease typing accuracy but also speed. Try to type all words. If a mistype happens, do not try to use Backspace; just keep typing. Erasing will waste your time and it cannot be more fruitful than typing the rest of the text carefully. You could invest this time by slowing down your speed for a while to achieve high accuracy and speed.

7. Act as You Type

You will see a progress report as you type. Be proactive and act accordingly. If accuracy is dropping too much, it means you have mistyped. Slow down your speed for a few seconds, say 30 seconds, and type as accurately as you can. In case the progress report shows a low speed, accelerate your fingers, just like you drive a car for a party or for picking someone up from the airport and you are getting there late.

TYPING AND FORMATTING TEXT

Typing and formatting text should be done separately. If typist tries to format the text as he types, then he will waste his precious time. It also reduces typing performance, speed and accuracy.

The best idea is to type all the text first and then format it in another go.

The reason is that the human brain can focuses only on one task at a time. Typist who does a single task at a time i.e. just typing can achieve high performance and pay attention to detail in later steps.

In my opinion, trying to correct any spelling, grammar or punctuation error at this stage is not fruitful.

I have noticed many typists who struggle to type a single word for three or four times because they want to fix the errors as they type. They are eager to do so.

You cannot imagine how badly it affects the typing speed and accuracy.

As final words just keep typing without taking into account typos, formatting and spelling or grammar mistakes. The idea is very simple, one task at a time. This will greatly simplify your job and could help you improve your efficiency.

This way you can quit the habit of typing one-word, time and again due to live typos corrections.

GETTING NERVOUS WHEN TOUCH TYPING

Oh, The Boss is Coming, or the trainer is looking at me, or even a colleague is observing my typing speed.

In the riskiest case, the zombie is coming. I need to type fast and accurately at any cost.

In many situations such as listed above, a touch typist gets nervous just because of the presence of a boss, manager, a coworker and so forth.

When touch typing, and in the meanwhile someone like a director, supervisor or even collaborator comes in, you will get puzzled and ultimately you will not perform better or in some cases, it can be termed as the worst performance of the day.

You will care too much to not commit mistakes and type as well as possible but believe me you will not be able to type with your normal speed and accuracy. Do not worry at all, it is a normal marvel and unluckily it can't be completely taken out.

Anyhow, one can overcome this fear by keeping up the following tips.

Do Not Get Nervous

Don't get nervous that you will perform badly. Give yourself the incentive that you can type well in front of anyone. Don't panic, relax, start typing and gradually increase your typing speed.

Type Infront of People

When someone surrounds you, type as much as possible. Don't fear while working in the presence of boss, executive or co-worker. They are also human beings like you, except for other positions. To err is human; It is normal if you make typos or can't reach a certain accuracy while working beside your boss, manager or workfellow.

Never Go for Over Performance

Don't try to over perform. Just stick with your normal speed and accuracy. Yes, you can show your talent when you are a typing guru or very expert to do so.

VOICE TYPING

It is a fact that touch typing is very useful on a keyboard but at the same time, it becomes useless on a touchscreen and smartphones. For touchscreens and smartphones, one finger typing is useful. For a full touch typist, it is very irritating and frustrating to type on touchscreen and smartphones. In other words, there are a lot of miss-hits for a touch typist on a touchscreen. On the off chance, a considerable amount of text is to be typed, it demands a lot of time and gets very frustrating.

The good news is that we can deal with this situation by using voice typing. Voice typing is a way in which spoken words are converted into written words. It is also known as speech-to-text. Voice typing can be easily employed on a smartphone without dogfight. Just tap the microphone icon and you are done. Voice typing capabilities will enable you to work faster and efficiently.

Google Voice Typing

Every one of us, sometimes or always have a good experience with voice typing on smartphones but what about touchscreen devices running on Windows or Mac operating systems. Their built-in voice recognition features cannot perform the conversion process efficiently. There comes google voice typing to rescue for voice typing on Windows or Mac. The Google Docs has an amazing voice typing capability and supports about 48 languages and the list keeps growing.

Here is how to start voice typing in Google Docs.

1. Launch Google Chrome browser.
2. Go to Google Docs by visiting ***https://docs.google.com***
3. Click on Blank.
4. Click the Tools menu and choose Voice Typing (or Press Ctrl+Shift+S).
5. Click on the Mic icon and start speaking.

Voice Typing vs Touch Typing

Voice typing cannot beat regular touch typing in speed and accuracy. Voice typing requires an environment where there is not a lot of noise and background sounds. In addition to this, a bad accent or pronunciation leads to incorrect written words. For example, voice typing cannot plainly distinguish among the words; there, their and dear but one can adapt to voice typing as time passes.

TYPING MATHEMATICAL EQUATIONS

Typing equations is a complex task and requires more attention as compared to normal typing because it involves numbers, special symbols and characters. Thoroughly formatting equations adds to the complexity and makes it a clumsy task for newbies.

You may have a bad experience if you have attempted typing mathematics assignment for the first time.

The easiest way to write equations is to use Microsoft Word Native Equation Editor or Mathtype software. Microsoft Word native equations editor is an easy to reach tool for entering simple and complex equations. On the other hand, Mathtype is a powerful equation editor with interactive interface. It is available for Windows and Macintosh operating systems. It has an enormous set of symbols and special characters which allows user to type mathematical equations and formulas for various purposes such as word processing, presentation, learning, publishing TeX, MathML and LaTeX.

To be honest, Microsoft Word native equations editor has been built on Mathtype foundation and has never been updated for a long period of time. Hence, there are some limitations with Microsoft Word native equations editor.

The third option is to use latex and formulate equations. It is merely a programming language designed for writing complex documents, particularly documents with a lot of mathematical equations and graphs etc. It is not recommended for rookies to go with latex as it involves codes for every symbol.

Typing Mathematical Equation in Microsoft Word

Here are the steps to type mathematical equations in Microsoft Word.

1. Click on the **INSERT** tab.
2. Click on "Insert Equation" and then choose the "Insert New Equation" command.
3. Type your equation in "Type New Equation Here" box.

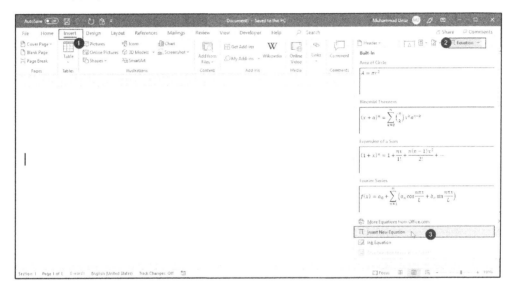

As a shortcut key you can use Alt and = keys combinations to insert equations instantly. If you are on a tablet, employ the ink Equation Tool to quickly insert equations into Microsoft word.

Typing equations using Mathtype Software

1. Launch Mathtype software.
2. Type equation in the Mathtype interface
3. Click on "Edit" menu and choose "Select All" command or press Ctrl + A
4. Click on "Edit" menu again and choose "Copy" command or press Ctrl + C

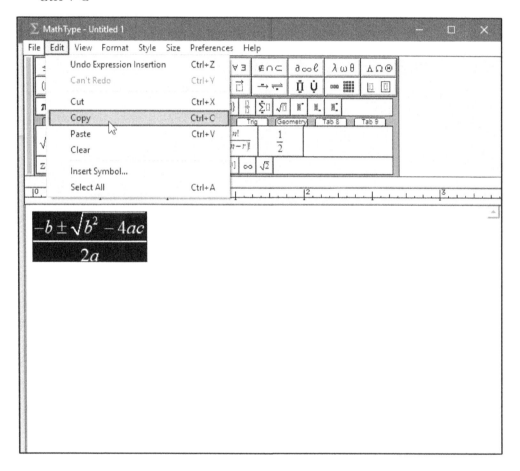

5. Now switch to Word Document.
6. Click on the "**Home**" tab.
7. Click on "Paste" option or press **Ctrl+V.**

Congratulations

You have successfully completed the *Touch Typing* course. You have walked a long way toward this goal and finally you have made it.

Thank you so much for reading and following my book!

Grab your own copy here:
https://www.amazon.com/dp/1729483046

DID THIS BOOK IMPROVE YOUR TYPING SKILLS?

Let me know how this book has improved your typing skill. Please, spare a few minutes for me to answer the following questions. I personally read emails, comments and suggestions. You can reach me through **Email**, **Social Media** or **Website**.

- Which part or lesson of this book you liked the most?
- Which lesson or part of this book you liked the least?
- Did you face any difficulty following it?
- What was your typing speed before following this book?
- What is your current typing speed?
- Do you have any other suggestions or comments? Please let me know.

You can check your typing speed here.

Typing12.com/typing-speed-test

Let me know your comments and suggestions.

	info@Typing12.com
	Typing12.com
	Facebook.com/TouchTyping12Lessons
	Twitter.com/Typing12Lessons
	Instagram.com/TouchTyping12Lessons
	Pinterest.com/TouchTyping12Lessons
	+92(0)3149090001
	TouchTyping.tumblr.com

About the Author

Muhammad Umar is a tech savvy utilizes modern technologies for teaching and learning purposes. He is passionate in helping students and professionals to grasp the basic concepts of Computer and Mathematics in an easier and practical way. He has been teaching Computer and Mathematics at primary and secondary levels. Every day, he steps into the classrooms with a strong belief in education and helps students and learners to reach their potential in attainment of their goals.

The author holds a master's degree in Computer Science with a major in Database. He is the founder of ***www.typing12.com*** and ***www.basicscomp.com*** and published more than 200 articles online. He has written three books on the subject 'Computer Education', published by Talent Publishers. He can be reached at.

umar@typing12.com

OTHER BOOKS BY THE SAME AUTHOR

- **BASICS OF COMPUTER**

 Basics of Computer, Third Edition, eradicates any intimidation about the computer. With a little investment of time, you will soon be able to understand basic concepts and perform simple tasks on your computer. The chapter-wise approach provides navigation through the contents, easy to grasp the language, clear technical definitions, and appropriate illustrations provide an understandable read to students.

ISBN: 978-1717044105

- **ONE LINE A DAY – A THREE YEAR JOURNAL**

One Line a Day - A Three Year Journal is a custom wider lines three years journal which keep you on track with memories of previous events. This journal is a great tool to replay thoughts and memories you had in your life. It allows you to write an entry for each day of the year and span over three years.

ISBN: 978-1794758094

- **QUICK TABLES 30+ EVERGREEN TABLES For Quick and Easy Reference**

This quick-witted booklet includes 30-plus tables which will make your life easier. It is small enough to fit into a pocket and you can carry it along. These zippy reference tables help students, engineers, teachers and professionals to outshine their classmates, friends and coworkers.

ISBN: 978-1717834232

- **100 DAYS OF MULTIPLICATION FACTS PROBLEMS:**

100 Days of Multiplication Facts Problems has 6000 multiplication facts problems for daily practice and focuses on digits 0-20.

There are 100 worksheets each having 60 problems. Date, time, and score can be tracked at the top of every page. To make the students fluent with multiplication facts and recall them without delay, several problems are repeated, or the digits are switched. Answers and multiplication facts charts are included at the end of the book, so that the students can check their answers easily.

ISBN: 979-8745290107

Made in the USA
Coppell, TX
20 August 2021